Motivational Interviewing
and
Stages of Change

Motivational Interviewing
and
Stages of Change

Integrating Best Practices for
Substance Abuse Professionals

Kathyleen M. Tomlin, M.S., L.P.C., C.A.D.C. III

and Helen Richardson

Hazelden
Center City, Minnesota 55012-0176

1-800-328-9000
1-651-213-4590 (Fax)
www.hazelden.org

To request permission, write to Permissions Coordinator, Hazelden, P.O. Box 176, Center City, MN 55012-0176. To purchase additional copies of this publication, call 1-800-328-9000 or 1-651-213-4000.

ISBN: 1-59285-085-5

08 07 06 05 04   6 5 4 3 2 1

Cover design by David Spohn
Interior design and typesetting by Kinne Design

CONTENTS

ACKNOWLEDGMENTS

We wish to thank many people for the assistance and encouragement they offered us during the preparation of this book. Of special note are Phil Anderson, Jeff Beatty, Peggy Hickey, Ron Hunt, and Carol Morais, who work with clients every day. Their experience, knowledge, skill, and special efforts to teach and learn from each other and share their knowledge with us added immeasurably to this work.

Sherwin Moscow was the originator of the At-a-Glance sheets. These pages assist counselors with integration of the theory and nomenclature of MI/SOC. Karen Kahle spent hours assisting us to perfect the earlier chapters, which offer a conceptual basis for the book.

Susan Hayashi, Ph.D., and Judy Huang, Ph.D., contributed to the agency level implementation section found in appendix B. Their hard work created an implementation plan that counselors will find useful in their work with clients. Our colleague Dave Mason allowed us to reproduce his program's MI/SOC implementation plan as an example for readers' benefit. Kathy Laws's editing comments and suggestions were most beneficial in creating an implementation section that is user friendly and practical for counselors.

Miguel Tellez graciously allowed us to use his culturally based activities. Miguel's work with young people in the development and execution of these activities has led to resources we believe the reader will find most effective. John Hahn proposed and helped refine the multiple family activity entitled Consequences of Using.

Gloria Henricks's expertise as a graphic artist, in addition to her experience in working with substance-abusing clients, contributed to the creation of the MI/SOC-based treatment plan. Jeff White also provided valuable assistance with graphics.

Dan Dickinson was instrumental in creating and refining the ratings sheets for counselor practice. He also provided conceptual and editing assistance through the development of portions of the book.

Our thanks also go to our editor, Richard Solly, for assisting us to stay on task, encouraging us, and offering important critical feedback to improve this work.

We are indebted to the creators and authors of the Transtheoretical Model of Change and Motivational Interviewing for their dedicated work. They have made immense contributions increasing the ability of clinicians to significantly improve their clinical work.

Finally, we extend a special note of thanks to the countless clients who have shared their experiences in treatment and efforts toward recovery. Their courage has inspired us to offer this book to the substance abuse field for consideration and out of respect for their journey toward change.

■ ■ ■

INTRODUCTION

This book is the result of many years of working with people struggling with substance abuse and dependence, as well as the professionals who help them recover and make healthy changes in their lives. The material in it includes ideas and activities that have been thoroughly tested by counselors in clinical practice and others who have used them in a variety of settings, as well as by researchers working in programs. The material is currently being used successfully in a variety of settings (substance abuse, criminal justice, mental health, and health care, including inpatient and outpatient) with a variety of clients, including youth, adults, dual-diagnosed, males and females, and people of various cultures and ethnicities. Practitioners have found the version we present here to be both practical and useful. Numerous clinics have chosen to adopt this method as one of the best ways they have of working with their clients. As clinicians use this framework with yet more clients in various settings, we fully expect it to grow and evolve. We hope it will be valuable to you and aid you in advancing the treatment of substance abuse.

Over the last decades, the addictions field has grown and changed dramatically. Throughout the years, people have sought to help individuals suffering from addiction find positive, drug-free lifestyles. The book *Slaying the Dragon: The History of Addiction Treatment and Recovery in America* by William L. White contains a thorough presentation of this rich history for those who are interested. From time to time, new approaches have come to the forefront and contributed significantly to existing treatment.

Two well-researched approaches, the Transtheoretical Model of Stages of Change (SOC) and Motivational Interviewing (MI), have emerged lately. Although their development began some time ago, they have come into prominence more recently. While treatment providers are beginning to use SOC and MI with their clients and are implementing them in their programming, change can be challenging even for the most motivated. We see that daily

Duplicating this page is illegal. Do not copy this material without written permission from the publisher.

1

when working with clients. The same is true for programs and agencies that serve clients with substance abuse. The introduction of new practices to an existing program, even ones based on research that hold promise for improving client outcomes, is not always readily embraced.

This book is written for counselors who work in a clinical setting with people experiencing substance abuse and addiction. While the concepts discussed can be applied to short-term contact between client and helper, our focus is on the practitioner who develops an ongoing counseling relationship with substance-abusing and addicted people. It is our belief and experience that blending the philosophy, concepts, and skills of MI with the theoretical orientation of SOC results in a clinical framework that allows clinicians to individualize care as they guide each client along the path of change. By following the theory of SOC and utilizing MI's counseling style, skill set, and strategies, the practitioner can "operationalize," or put into practice, the stages theory. This blending of the two models provides a road map sensitive to the process of change while also providing direction for interventions most likely to move clients along their path toward recovery.

For readers who are new to this material, we have included a summary of the fundamentals of both Motivational Interviewing and Stages of Change. For those who are more familiar with these concepts, the summary may serve as a reminder of what you already know. For both sets of readers, information about how the processes of change function with SOC and interact with MI may be new. The way in which their interrelationship is conceptualized and presented in this book may provide you with insight into how they work together and how to use them in practice.

Readers will notice that we have emphasized the attitudes and approaches counselors take as they deal with their clients. We believe it is extremely important to understand the significance of the counseling *style* basic to the MI approach. The skills and techniques embodied in MI can be used with many counseling styles. However, this book proposes a blend of MI with SOC that assumes an MI counseling style. It is therefore important for readers to evaluate how congruent this style is with their own beliefs and approaches to counseling.

Additional resources and a bibliography are included to guide readers who wish to further explore topics of interest to them. Since the English language has not yet devised a gender-free way of referring to individuals, we have chosen to use male and female pronouns interchangeably throughout this book.

■ ■ ■

ACTIVITIES LIST

Throughout this book, you'll find numerous treatment activities to use with your clients and special populations, such as teens, people from culturally diverse backgrounds, and clients suffering with co-occurring disorders. Most of the activities presented throughout the book can be adapted for other groups of clients with little effort from the reader. The activities will help you understand and practice the skills and concepts presented. There also are practical tools for the reader to use in counseling sessions. We encourage you to take the time to use these activities. They will help you internalize the information and techniques and further your understanding of how MI and SOC work together.

The format of chapters 3 through 5 is organized in the same way. Each chapter contains an introduction, a summary of the stages of change and the goals for each stage, and a table listing stages of change, processes of change, and motivational strategies for counselors. The tables are adapted from *Enhancing Motivation for Change in Substance Abuse Treatment Programs,* one of a Treatment Improvement Protocol Series (TIP 35) produced by the Substance Abuse and Mental Health Services Administration.

Each chapter also contains activities for you to use with clients. The activities are numbered and contain a box in which the relevant stage of change, processes of change, and complementary MI skills and strategies are identified. The box also contains counseling setting application suggestions. You'll find Activity Steps for implementing each activity and an Activity Application section, which outlines the rationale of, thoughts about, or details of the activities as you apply them in your practice. A list of the activities by chapter and title can be found on the next page.

In the final chapter, we discuss the additional challenges facing counselors, supervisors, and agencies as they begin to use the approach we describe. We offer here and in the appendixes materials and tools for guidance and practical application in this aspect of the process of change.

CHAPTER ACTIVITIES

FUNDAMENTALS

The meaning of things lies not in the things
themselves but in our attitude towards them.

— ANTOINE DE SAINT-EXUPÉRY

Substance abuse professionals continually strive to improve the quality of care for clients. As practitioners, we regularly encounter new methods of treatment possibilities. For years practitioners in the substance abuse field have been concerned with the high rates of client recidivism as well as the lack of client retention, client resistance, and other issues that leave staff feeling inadequate. As a result, we look for and encounter an array of treatment approaches designed to maximize client success.

Research offers insight into what works in general for a majority of people. Research can tell us what has made a difference for specific groups of people under controlled sets of circumstances. For instance, studies have compared the effect of elements such as clinician style and number of treatment options offered on factors such as retention in treatment and reduction in substance use. Helping us put the best available ideas into practice, research can validate what we do well and point out what we need to further incorporate into our practice.

On the next page is a grid and quiz that explore commonly held beliefs in our field. As you read the statements, check whether you believe them to be true or false.

BELIEFS ABOUT PRACTICE	True	False
1. The most important factor in treatment outcomes is whether or not the client expects he can succeed in changing.		
2. A client's motivation to change depends primarily on internal factors such as distress levels, self-esteem, and awareness of the impact of use on others.		
3. The quality of the counselor-client relationship is key to client satisfaction and change.		
4. Most clients enter treatment in denial.		
5. It is the counselor's job to confront the client's denial in order for the client to see that her use is a problem.		
6. How a counselor feels about a client's chances of success affects client outcomes.		

Following are the answers to the above statements with the corresponding research that supports, counters, or modifies the statements.

1. The most important factor in treatment outcomes is whether or not the client expects he can succeed in changing.

Answer: False.

Research says: A review and analysis of forty years of research studies and more than four hundred therapeutic models identified four fundamental and common factors that account for the effectiveness of treatment across treatment modalities.[1] The four factors are *the clients themselves, the therapeutic relationship, expectancy,* and *theoretical orientation.*

Researchers found that who the client is (including his surrounding environment and circumstances and his belief in the possibility of change) and the relationship that develops between the client and the clinician are likely to have the most influence on increasing the probability of a positive treatment outcome. Other factors—expectancy (how much clients expect that their therapy will work) and the therapist's theoretical orientation or technique—account for less than one-third of the effectiveness of treatment.

2. **A client's motivation to change depends primarily on internal factors such as distress levels, self-esteem, and awareness of the impact of use on others.**

   Answer: False.

Research says: Motivation to change varies depending on many factors. Some are internal, such as level of distress, self-esteem, or awareness of the impact of substance use on themselves or their families.[2] Others are external. Clients who have social supports are more likely to enter and remain in treatment.[3] Significant life changes such as marriage, traumatic events, and major illness can be the impetus for drug abusers to consider changing their use.[4] Prochaska even notes a case in which a couple who smoked heavily for a long time stopped smoking when their dog died of lung cancer. [5]

3. **The quality of the counselor-client relationship is key to client satisfaction and change.**

   Answer: True.

Research says: The therapeutic relationship plays an important role in facilitating change. The Project MATCH Research Group found a positive relationship between therapist behaviors and both client drinking behavior and client satisfaction.[6] Additional studies have found that counselors who display empathy, warmth, respect, and genuineness enhance the process of developing a therapeutic relationship; when they use a directive, controlling style of confrontation, client dropout rates increase and desirable outcomes decline.[7]

4. **Most clients enter treatment in denial.**

   Answer: False.

Research says: Not all clients exhibit symptoms of denial. Research reports that denial, as a defense mechanism, is no more common among the substance-abusing population than it is in the general population.[8] As you will see, when clients enter treatment, how they are treated affects their expressions of denial.

5. **It is the counselor's job to confront the client's denial in order for the client to see that her use is a problem.**

   Answer: False.

   Research says: The counselor's approach has a significant effect on client displays of denial. Numerous studies have shown that confrontational approaches lead to *increases* in resistance and denial and, in some cases, result in increased drinking by clients.[9]

6. **How a counselor feels about a client's chances of success affects client outcomes.**

   Answer: True.

   Research says: In many situations, people achieve what is expected of them. When counselors were told certain clients would probably be very successful in treatment, those clients (who were randomly picked) performed better in the opinions of both counselors and peers.[10]

■

After this brief overview, you may be wondering how you can use these research findings in your clinical practice. Though there are many directions in which to go, we really have only two options—staying the same or changing. We hope change is the option chosen and that programs and practitioners look to research findings as a resource for their development.

Today, much research points toward the two approaches that are the subject of this book—Stages of Change and Motivational Interviewing. In addition to the work previously cited, Project MATCH compared the effectiveness of various alcoholism treatment modalities and found that during the first year of the posttreatment period, a motivational treatment model was as effective as Twelve Step Facilitation and cognitive-behavioral models.[11]

Imagine, then, our excitement when we came upon the two approaches presented in this book. We have found that the Stages of Change concept included in the Transtheoretical Model of Change, together with the counseling style and philosophy of Motivational Interviewing, offers many successful outcomes. Blending these two approaches provides counselors with a framework with which to determine where a client is in the change process, and it also provides a range of tools and strategies that counselors can use with clients relevant to the stage of change identified.

From this background, we turn to a brief examination of Motivational Interviewing (MI) and Stages of Change (SOC) theory, both of which are in the process of evolving. For the purposes of this book, we will summarize the fundamentals only. Numerous books and articles have been written about MI and SOC, many of which are referenced in the notes and bibliography sections of this book (pages 223–29). We encourage readers to take advantage of this wealth of information to deepen and broaden their knowledge of these approaches to treatment.

■ ■ ■

Duplicating this page is illegal. Do not copy this material without written permission from the publisher.

11

INTEGRATING MOTIVATIONAL INTERVIEWING AND STAGES OF CHANGE

It is only by selection, by elimination, by emphasis
that we get to the real meaning of things.

— GEORGIA O'KEEFFE

Motivational Interviewing (MI) and Stages of Change (SOC) have been around in the treatment community and research world for some time now. The reader may be familiar with these models and be tempted to skip this section for the assignments and exercises in the remaining chapters. However, in this chapter we do offer counselors, even those thoroughly familiar with MI and SOC, new material, such as the Processes of Change and tips for implementing MI.

This chapter has four main sections: (1) a review of SOC, (2) a review of the Processes of Change, (3) a review of MI, and (4) integrating or combining SOC and MI. The material is organized and presented in convenient charts that offer a quick and easy reference for your daily work with clients.

Stages of Change Review

To begin our review of the Stages of Change, take a moment before reading on and answer the following question: Can you identify the six Stages of Change?

Answer: The illustration on the next page shows the six Stages of Change in the Prochaska, DiClemente, and Norcross model:

1. precontemplation
2. contemplation
3. preparation
4. action
5. maintenance
6. termination[1]

The SOC theory shows the process people go through when changing problematic behaviors, such as substance abuse. The stages are a pathway that people take through change at their own pace and timing. Following is a brief description of each stage, along with its primary components, and examples of how your clients might experience each stage.

Precontemplation Stage

In the precontemplation stage, people do not see their behavior as being a problem. Not even feedback from others about their negative behavior causes them to consider the negative impact of their alcohol or drug use. Precontemplators may say, "I don't have a problem with alcohol," or "I can control my use," or "I only use on the weekends," much to the frustration of those around them who experience the impact of the users' behavior. In this stage, smokers, for example, may ignore the effects of secondhand smoke on others, despite the pleas of those around them to stop smoking.

Contemplation Stage

Contemplators acknowledge the possibility that their substance use is problematic, but they are in the grips of ambivalence regarding their use. This ambivalence is the hallmark of contemplation. Clients acknowledge their need to change, but they aren't sure they really want to change. In this stage, contemplators may say, "I have thought about changing, but I'm not sure I need to right now," or "I feel so humiliated having to spend the night in jail, but it's hard to imagine not being able to drink again." Often in this stage of change, clients are struggling with two opposing core values.

Preparation Stage

In the preparation stage, people have made a decision to change. Clients in the preparation stage may say, "I've got to do something about this problem!" or "Things are going to be so much better once I'm off the booze." It is important to assist clients making concrete plans for change that result in a higher probability for success.

Decision to change

Action Stage

Clients display the greatest behavioral changes while in the action stage. As the word *action* implies, clients are actively implementing a plan for change. Overeaters will eliminate fatty foods from their environment; smokers will rid themselves of cigarettes or ashtrays; and people suffering from addiction will get rid of their drugs and any remaining drug paraphernalia. People usually need a lot of recognition and positive reinforcement during this stage, since their behavior is observable and clearly represents an achievement for themselves.

active implementation

Maintenance Stage

In the maintenance stage, clients have a high comfort level with their new behavior. It no longer preoccupies a major portion of their time. To stay in maintenance, clients need to continue monitoring gains they have made and follow their strategies to prevent relapse. They also need to update these strategies as they and their life situation change. In this stage, some people can lose sight of their relapse-prevention strategies and may experience a recurrence of old behaviors that could lead to a using event. If this happens and clients review and return to their relapse-prevention strategies, they continue to be in the maintenance stage.

comfort level and monitoring

Relapse occurs her more frequently

The authors of the Transtheoretical Model of Change see the process of relapse or recurrence of using as occurring during the maintenance stage of change. Relapse or return to use is not a phenomenon that happens to all individuals during the maintenance stage of change, but it is common enough for many to highlight this phenomenon. In other documents, the process of relapse or recurrence may occur as a separate stage, although typically occurring around the maintenance phase of change.[2]

Duplicating this page is illegal. Do not copy this material without written permission from the publisher.

15

Termination Stage

Problem Resolved

The termination stage of a problem behavior, like cigarette smoking or alcoholic drinking, is the stage in the change process at which the problem behavior is resolved. It is common for those who treat people with substance abuse to be cautious about this stage of change. In the theory, this stage is reached when the original change is no longer part of the clients' thinking, and they have less need to plan around managing their changes. For example, some smokers can reach termination and be immune from relapsing, while others may need to carefully monitor themselves indefinitely.

Now that we have reviewed SOC, let's do another activity. Following are statements people often say in various stages of change. See if you can match the statement with the correct stage of change.

STATEMENT	Stage of Change (SOC)
1. I am ready to make a plan to address my alcohol use.	
2. My family is on my back. I know I need to get this DUI figured out, but it's too much trouble. Besides, my drinking is not a problem for me. I drink like everybody else I know.	
3. I have been clean for the last eight months with no problems. Although I had thoughts about using, I worked through them and felt good about it.	
4. I really would like to keep my friends who still use, but I am finding that if I hang out with them, I end up drinking again.	
5. Smoking? I haven't thought about smoking for years!	
6. Changing my drug use, especially marijuana, has turned out to be one of the best things I have ever done. I would have never believed that a few months ago.	

Answers:

1. SOC: *Preparation*

   This client wants to change, though he indicates he may need help making a plan to change.

2. SOC: *Precontemplation*

   For this client, drinking and driving isn't regarded as much of a problem. She does not see her use as problematic. Thus, she is in precontemplation about her use.

3. SOC: *Maintenance*

   As this statement indicates, the client has been successful in not using for eight months. He most likely will be open to continuing to manage relapse symptoms.

4. SOC: *Contemplation*

   This client is experiencing mixed feelings about making lifestyle changes, which is the hallmark of contemplation.

5. SOC: *Termination*

   Although not commonly referred to in the addictions field, the termination stage describes a person who has completed a process of change on a long-term basis. This client has integrated the choice to stop smoking to the extent that she no longer sees it as a problem.

6. SOC: *Action*

   Experiencing successful change is common in the action stage of change.

Processes of Change Review

As an adjunct to the Stages of Change, the authors have added a list entitled the Processes of Change.[3] These ten processes or variables further distinguish what happens to people as they go through behavior change. Some of these processes are *experiential,* meaning a person experiences an event that creates a new way of thinking and feeling that, in turn, leads to change. Other processes are *behavioral,* consisting of activities that reinforce the changes that people are making.

The list on the next page identifies the most current processes of change along with the letter *E* or *B* to denote if the process is primarily experiential or behavioral. The name of each process of change is stated in the original research terminology and defined. As you read the list, try to identify which stage of change is most applicable to the process of change.

1. *Consciousness raising (E)*

   A person becomes aware, which requires him to learn something new about behaviors that need to be changed.

2. *Social liberation (E, B)*

   A person recognizes changes in society that make it easier to follow through with the changes she is personally making or wants to make.

3. *Emotional arousal (E)*

   A person experiences an intensely charged event that results in movement toward change.

4. *Self-reevaluation (E)*

   A person experiences something that causes him to reflect on personal goals and values related to his use of substances.

5. *Stimulus control (B)*

   A person learns to manage barriers to change, such as triggers, and develops new coping skills to maintain change.

6. *Helping relationships (E, B)*

   A person identifies a variety of supportive people to help reinforce the desired changes.

7. *Reinforcement management (B)*

   A person regularly celebrates progress toward change.

8. *Counterconditioning (B)*

   A person chooses new ways to behave and interact to support the desired change.

9. *Self-liberation (B)*

   A person creates a plan that moves her to permanent change.

10. *Environmental reevaluation (E)*

    A person evaluates how his use affects home, friends, work, and other lifestyle areas.

So how does this fit together? The table below lists client statements from the exercise on page 16. Can you identify *one* process of change (POC) for each statement in the chart? Write your answer in the space provided.

TIP:

The experiential processes of change often occur in the early stages of change, and the behavioral processes come later.

STATEMENT	SOC and POC
1. I am ready to make a plan to address my alcohol use.	SOC: *Preparation* POC:
2. My family is on my back. I know I need to get this DUI figured out, but it's too much trouble. Besides, my drinking is not a problem for me. I drink like everybody else I know.	SOC: *Precontemplation* POC:
3. I have been clean for the last eight months with no problems. Although I had thoughts about using, I worked through them and felt good about it.	SOC: *Maintenance* POC:
4. I really would like to keep my friends who still use, but I am finding that if I hang out with them, I end up drinking again.	SOC: *Contemplation* POC:
5. Smoking? I haven't thought about smoking for years!	SOC: *Termination* POC:
6. Changing my drug use, especially marijuana, has turned out to be one of the best things I have ever done. I would have never believed that a few months ago.	SOC: *Action* POC:

How did you do? In the illustration below, the stages of change are paired with the processes of change where they are most likely to operate together. To answer the quiz on page 19, compare your responses to this illustration. Note that the experiential processes of change relate primarily to the precontemplation and contemplation stages, and the behavioral processes relate primarily to the later stages.

Stages of Change

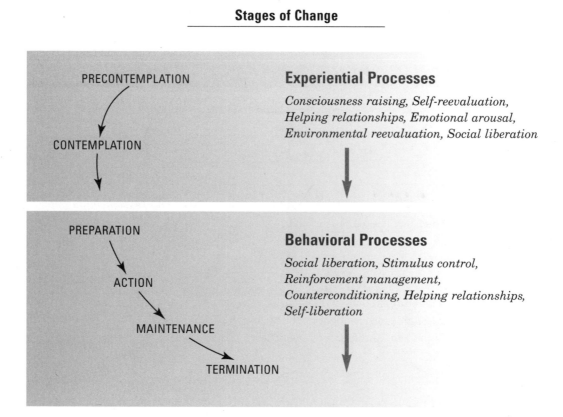

PRECONTEMPLATION

CONTEMPLATION

Experiential Processes

Consciousness raising, Self-reevaluation, Helping relationships, Emotional arousal, Environmental reevaluation, Social liberation

PREPARATION

ACTION

MAINTENANCE

TERMINATION

Behavioral Processes

Social liberation, Stimulus control, Reinforcement management, Counterconditioning, Helping relationships, Self-liberation

The Stages of Change and Processes of Change described above provide a straightforward, well-documented view of behavior change, which is of great value to clients and clinicians. The Transtheoretical Model enables clinicians to further refine techniques and interventions that can best empower the client and maximize chances of success. Understanding the stages and processes of change helps one understand how change works and what can get in the way of change. The critical task for clients and clinicians, however, is to find a way to bring this theory into practice. The next section outlines the basic concepts of Motivational Interviewing and how to put this theory of change to work, at the same time that one is incorporating the use of the Transtheoretical Model.

Motivational Interviewing Review

The individual Motivational Interviewing (MI) skills needed are not unusual in the counseling field. Clinicians commonly think that they are already practicing MI since most clinical training encompasses basic counseling skills such as active listening, use of open-ended questions, use of affirmations, and summarizing. What makes MI a unique counseling approach is how its skills are employed by clinicians. MI requires attention to timing issues, specific strategies and application methods, and maximizing the effectiveness of these skills in your work to support clients' change.

MI is a philosophical approach that includes a unique counseling and communication style. As such, it can be used in combination with other therapeutic approaches. William Miller and Stephen Rollnick define MI as "a client-centered, directive method for enhancing intrinsic motivation to change by exploring and resolving ambivalence."[4] MI engages the therapist as an empathic partner who creates a collaborative environment in which clients are not judged but accepted, empowered, supported, and understood. MI encompasses several key concepts from other theories such as Rogerian, cognitive-behavioral, and social learning models of counseling.

It's critical to know the *primary principles* of MI: express empathy, develop discrepancy, roll with resistance, and support self-efficacy. See the chart on pages 22–23 for further clarification. In addition, MI has two phases that the counselor needs to understand and employ to assist client change: Phase 1—*building motivation* for change—and Phase 2—*strengthening commitment* to change. Each of these phases contains specific skills and strategies that support the principles and practice of MI and reinforce how the counselor interacts with clients.

Four basic skills form the foundation of Phase 1, building motivation. The skills are known by the acronym *OARS,*[5] which stands for *open-ended questions, affirmation, reflections,* and *summary.* Their definitions appear in the chart on pages 22–23. OARS skills are used in different combinations and in certain ways to build what Miller and Rollnick call rapport, establish trust, and create a client-centered environment effectively. OARS skills reduce resistance while communicating to clients that they are heard, understood, and acknowledged for the choices they are making.

The strategies of Phase 2, strengthening commitment, build on the clients' motivation and resolve to change. While continuing to use OARS, the MI counselor adds the strategies of assessing readiness, making a transitional summary (recapitulation), asking key questions, offering information and advice, and negotiating change plans to help clients move along the stages of change and deeper into Phase 2.[6]

The chart that follows identifies, defines, and integrates the principles mentioned above with Phase 1 and 2 strategies and skills. Reflective listening, listed under the heading Phase 1 Strategies/Skills, is another important MI skill to learn. Following the chart, there is a section entitled Reflective Listening Examples. This section contains reflective listening examples a counselor might make to a client.

MI PRINCIPLES	Phase I Strategies / Skills	Phase 2 Strategies / Skills
Express Empathy Expressing empathy includes communicating acceptance "through skillful reflective listening"[7] that helps clients explore and resolve their confusion about impending changes without fear of embarrassment or shame.	*Open-Ended Questions* Ask open-ended questions to develop relationships with clients by inviting them to give more than simple one-word answers. For example, ask, "What brought you here today?" or "How can I be helpful to you today?"	*Readiness to Change* Assessing clients' readiness to change is important when evaluating what interventions are appropriate to help them move forward. Using an inappropriate intervention may create resistance in clients and slow progress or result in client dropout, an undesirable though common phenomenon.
Develop Discrepancy Developing discrepancy creates doubt for the client about the consistency between personal values he has expressed and current behavior. When the counselor does this with skill, the client in fact ends up confronting himself, perhaps the most meaningful form of confrontation.	*Affirmation* Affirming a client involves making positive statements that support and focus on her strengths, constructive actions, and efforts to change. Affirmations build confidence and hope for clients, reinforcing their self-efficacy. Statements such as "Congratulations on completing your assignments; I know this is something you have.	*Transitional Summary and Key Questions* Typically, these two strategies are most useful when clients are transitioning between the contemplation stage and the preparation stage. Transitional summaries include information about the client's view of the situation, the counselor's assessment, objective information, and the client's comments indicating a desire to change.

MI PRINCIPLES	Phase 1 Strategies / Skills	Phase 2 Strategies / Skills
Develop Discrepancy *continued*	been working hard to accomplish" or "Thanks for taking time to check in today" are examples of affirmations.	Key questions such as "What do you think you might do?" help the client get concrete about his next steps.
Roll with Resistance Decreased resistance leads to better treatment outcomes. Following the principle of rolling with resistance, the client begins to argue for her own need to change. The client-counselor relationship is seen as a critical collaboration. The emergence of resistance is a cue for the counselor to respond to the client in a manner that avoids increasing resistance while maintaining a collaborative environment.	*Reflective Listening* Reflective listening is basic to practicing MI effectively. Reflections are statements that indicate counselors heard what the client said or meant to convey. Making reflective statements requires that counselors set aside their pre-conceived notions about what clients need and instead focus on understanding what their clients are trying to get across. To do this, counselors adopt an approach that involves making a hypothesis about what clients want to communicate and then testing that hypothesis by making a reflective statement. Examples of reflective listening follow this chart.	*Information and Advice* Although MI counselors hesitate to give advice, there are times when information and advice are what clients need. There are times when clients sincerely do not know what options are available or lack concrete information about something, such as how to make a budget. While it is important for counselors to avoid telling clients what to do, it is acceptable to offer suggestions or advice when clients are ready to receive it.
Support Self-Efficacy Miller and Rollnick define *self-efficacy* as "a person's belief in his or her ability to carry out and succeed with a specific task."[8] The concept of self-efficacy is borrowed from social learning theory, particularly from the work of Alfred Bandura.	*Summary* Summary statements are used to bring together information at various points in the therapeutic relationship. A summary highlights concerns of the client, brings out doubts or ambivalence about change, and points out discrepancies between what the client says and how the client behaves.	*Negotiating a Change Plan* Planning for change is important in increasing the probability that clients will be successful. Counselors can help clients negotiate a change plan by assisting them to prepare plans carefully, ensuring they are both practical and realistic.

Reflective Listening Examples

1. *Client statement:*

   My wife thinks I drink too much, but I really do not think it is a problem.

   Counselor reflective response:

   You're not concerned about your use, but you know your wife has concerns. (Client is heard. Counselor repeats what the client says.)

2. *Client statement:*

   Dad made me come here. I like to drink and smoke pot, but don't care if I change or not.

   Counselor reflective response:

   Your father wants you to change, but you have already made up your mind not to change. (Client is heard. Counselor adds more to the client statement that the client has not said, but may have implied.)

3. *Client statement:*

   I'm here because I got caught at work with a positive drug screen for marijuana. I resent having to lose job time and go through this. I am never high on the job, and what I do on the weekend is my business.

   Counselor reflective response:

   Taking the time to come to this appointment is really upsetting to you. It sounds like you feel put upon by having to be here. Also, you resent the implication that your work is suffering as a result of your occasional use of marijuana. (Client is heard. Counselor interprets and adds more meaning to what the client has said.)

Change Talk

One final Phase 1 skill that merits special attention is *change talk*.[9] Change talk is a key directive strategy of MI. Counselors can use change talk strategies to move clients along the process of change by skillfully exploring and extracting clients' reasons to change while acknowledging their reasons not to move toward change. Researchers have demonstrated it is the strength of client commitment talk that is the most significant predictor of change.[10]

The counselor elicits change talk using the desires, abilities, reasons, and needs of the client as well as capitalizing on the client's important values and strengths. From there, the counselor attends to the client's readiness for moving toward change. As the client talks more about what he might change, how he might change, and when change will happen for him, the more likely that the client will actually change. There are additional strategies that work with the concept of change talk, such as exploring goals and values or identifying pros and cons for change, which are explored more thoroughly in chapter 6 of William Miller and Stephen Rollnick's *Motivational Interviewing,* 2d edition (see bibliography). In appendix A, there is further discussion about the nature of change talk, including a diagram that depicts the process of using change talk strategically.

Let's look at client statements made earlier in this chapter, as well as some others. Note what MI skills and strategies you'd suggest for each statement. Write your responses in the space provided.

CLIENT STATEMENT	MI SKILL AND STRATEGY
1. I am here to get a plan so that I can satisfy the judge and get on with my life. I am tired of being controlled by other people and want it to stop.	
2. I would like to stay out of trouble with my family regarding my substance abuse problems, but every time I try, I fail. So I just keep using.	

continued on next page

CLIENT STATEMENT	MI SKILL AND STRATEGY
3. I have been clean for the last eight months with no problems. Although I had thoughts about using, I worked through them and felt good about it.	
4. I really would like to keep my friends who still use, but I am finding that if I hang out with them, I end up drinking again.	
5. Smoking? I haven't thought about smoking for years!	
6. So far I am happy about the changes I have made. Seeing the successes thus far is encouraging me to look at other aspects of my life.	

Now compare your responses with those suggested below.

CLIENT STATEMENT	MI SKILL AND STRATEGY
1. I am here to get a plan so that I can satisfy the judge and get on with my life. I am tired of being controlled by other people and want it to stop.	• Reinforce the commitment to change by asking the client to elaborate more on his reasons to change. • Affirm client for taking charge of his situation. • Use OARS throughout the session. • Negotiate a change plan if appropriate.
2. I would like to stay out of trouble with my family regarding my substance abuse problems, but every time I try, I fail. So I just keep using.	• Build relationship and rapport with the client. • Listen well—reflect and ask open-ended questions, using OARS. • Ask permission to explore the client's concerns. • Offer hope for change.
3. I have been clean for the last eight months with no problems. Although I had thoughts about using, I worked through them and felt good about it.	• Revisit plan for change. • Normalize relapse. • Provide encouragement. • Explore barriers and assist in problem solving them.
4. I really would like to keep my friends who still use, but I am finding that if I hang out with them, I end up drinking again.	• Explore conflicting values. • Identify and build strengths. • Normalize ambivalence. • Elicit and reinforce change talk, using OARS.
5. Smoking? I haven't thought about smoking for years!	• Affirm ongoing commitment to behavior change.
6. So far I am happy about the changes I have made. Seeing the successes thus far is encouraging me to look at other aspects of my life.	• Continue to monitor readiness for continued change. • Affirm success. • Assist with issues related to carrying out plans for change as needed. • Offer information/advice as identified by the client. • Use OARS.

Traps and Hazards

Miller and Rollnick have identified particular pitfalls, called "traps" in Phase 1[11] and "hazards" in Phase 2.[12] The traps are question/answer, taking sides, expert, labeling, premature focus, and blaming. The hazards include overprescription, underestimating ambivalence, and insufficient direction. For a detailed review of them along with tips to avoid them, please refer to appendix A.

Combining Motivational Interviewing and Stages of Change

So far, we've reviewed the primary concepts of MI and SOC. What follows is our view of how these two approaches work together to provide a clear road map for clinical practice. The following grids identify the stages of change on the top. The first column lists the processes of change most likely involved, along with potential treatment goals for clients. The second column lists MI principles to guide counselors as they work with clients at each stage of change. The final column suggests MI strategies and skills counselors can use to accomplish the treatment goals chosen.

In creating this document, we purposefully omitted the termination stage as part of the treatment approach. A client in the termination stage would rarely request clinical services. Furthermore, we have found that many counselors do not believe that clients ever reach a termination stage of change. While some clients with different issues do reach a termination stage of treatment, more needs to be learned about this aspect of addiction to adequately address this stage of change.

Integrating Motivational Interviewing with Stages and Processes of Change

PRECONTEMPLATION STAGE

Clients do not see their behavior as a problem that needs changing.

PROCESSES OF CHANGE	MI PRINCIPLES	POTENTIAL MI STRATEGIES AND SKILLS
Consciousness Raising Increasing awareness about the effects of client's substance use on himself and others *Emotional Arousal* Emotional experiences that lead client to thinking about changing his substance use	*Express Empathy* *Roll with Resistance*	*Strategies* 1. Listen well to understand client issues from his perspective. 2. Remain client-centered. 3. Ask permission when exploring sensitive issues. 4. Ask for follow-up contact. 5. Respect client decisions regarding treatment. 6 Establish supportive counseling environment and relationship with client. 7. Explore client's motivation and confidence to change. *Skills* 1. Use OARS. 2. Avoid Phase 1 traps.

POTENTIAL TREATMENT GOALS

1. Establish supportive counseling environment and relationship with client.
2. Client will discover his motivation/confidence to change.
3. Evaluate client's substance use and obtain information to compare his use to objective standards.
4. Client will evaluate the current circumstances leading him to seek treatment.
5. Client will identify need for treatment.

Integrating Motivational Interviewing with Stages and Processes of Change *continued*

CONTEMPLATION STAGE

Clients are ambivalent about change.

PROCESSES OF CHANGE	MI PRINCIPLES	POTENTIAL MI STRATEGIES AND SKILLS
Environmental Reevaluation Looking at and reacting to client's external and internal experiences as they relate to changing substance use **Social Liberation** Identifying and utilizing the supports society offers to change substance use **Helping Relationships** Establishing supportive relationships while changing client's behavior related to substance use	*Express Empathy* *Develop Discrepancies* *Roll with Resistance* *Elicit Change Talk*	**Strategies** 1. Engage client in exploration of her goals and values for use/abstinence. 2. Identify client's strengths for change. 3. Normalize feelings of ambivalence. 4. Remain client-centered. 5. Empower client. 6. Explore both motivation and confidence. 7. Increase client's self-efficacy. 8. Help client explore discrepancies between values and goals. 9. Continue to build counseling relationship and environment. 10. Explore ambivalence. 11. Reinforce client's commitment to change. **Skills** 1. Use OARS. 2. Elicit change talk using change talk strategies. 3. Avoid Phase 1 traps.
POTENTIAL TREATMENT GOALS 1. Client will explore discrepancies between what she likes and dislikes about continuing or discontinuing her use. 2. Client will create a list of pros and cons for continued use. 3. Compare and contrast current behaviors with future goals for substance issues. 4. Client will discover her desires, needs, reasons, and abilities related to her current situation. 5. Client will identify her strengths for solving her dilemma regarding substance use.		

Integrating Motivational Interviewing with Stages and Processes of Change *continued*

PREPARATION STAGE

Clients decide to change but don't have a plan for it.

PROCESSES OF CHANGE	MI PRINCIPLES	POTENTIAL MI STRATEGIES AND SKILLS
Self-Liberation Experiencing hope and confidence in client's ability to address substance abuse issues **Social Liberation** Identifying and utilizing the supports society offers to change substance use **Helping Relationships** Establishing supportive relationships while changing client's behavior related to substance use	*Express Empathy* *Develop Discrepancy* *Roll with Resistance* *Eliciting Change Talk*	**Strategies** 1. Build client confidence. 2. Offer information and advice. 3. Discuss options. 4. Affirm client's decision making. 5. Continue to support client's self-efficacy. 6. Offer feedback on client's plan for change. **Skills** 1. Use OARS. 2. Offer transitional summary. 3. Avoid Phase 1 traps.
POTENTIAL TREATMENT GOALS 1. Client will identify changes he wants to make regarding his substance use. 2. Client will complete a written change plan. 3. Help client explore obstacles to achieving change goals. 4. Client will agree to ask others to support him in implementing plan.		

Duplicating this page is illegal. Do not copy this material without written permission from the publisher.

31

Integrating Motivational Interviewing with Stages and Processes of Change *continued*

<table>
<tr>
<td colspan="3">ACTION STAGE
Clients are implementing plans for change.</td>
</tr>
<tr>
<td>PROCESSES OF CHANGE</td>
<td>MI PRINCIPLES</td>
<td>POTENTIAL MI STRATEGIES AND SKILLS</td>
</tr>
<tr>
<td>

Counterconditioning
Creating options besides continued substance using

Reinforcement Management
Celebrating self for changing

Stimulus Control
Managing urges and triggers to use substances

Social Liberation
Identifying and utilizing the supports society offers to change substance use

Helping Relationships
Establishing supportive relationships while changing client's behavior related to substance use

</td>
<td>

Express Empathy

</td>
<td rowspan="2">

Strategies

1. Affirm client's effort to change.

2. Help client engage in resolving her substance abuse issues.

3. Encourage small steps toward change.

4. Identify new reinforcements for positive change.

5. Empower client.

6. Continue to assess readiness for change.

7. Offer assistance and guidance.

8. Reinforce hope.

Skills

1. Use OARS.

2. Use transitional summary to highlight for the client old versus new behaviors.

3. Avoid Phase 1 and 2 traps and hazards.

</td>
</tr>
<tr>
<td>

POTENTIAL TREATMENT GOALS

1. Help client explore success in making changes.

2. Reevaluate treatment plan and make changes as needed.

3. Client will identify ways to reward herself for the changes she makes.

4. Discuss urges and triggers to use along with possible solutions for avoiding them.

5. Client will identify and utilize the supports available to her in her community, such as Twelve Step meetings.

6. Client will maintain regular contact with clean and sober friends.

</td>
<td></td>
</tr>
</table>

Integrating Motivational Interviewing with Stages and Processes of Change *continued*

MAINTENANCE STAGE

Clients are maintaining change; some may need help with relapse prevention.

PROCESSES OF CHANGE	MI PRINCIPLES	POTENTIAL MI STRATEGIES AND SKILLS
Reinforcement Management Celebrating self for changing **Stimulus Control** Managing urges and triggers to use substances **Social Liberation** Identifying and utilizing the supports society offers to change substance use **Helping Relationships** Establishing supportive relationships while changing client's behavior related to substance use	*Express Empathy*	**Strategies** 1. Support self-efficacy. 2. Build on client's resolves to maintain long-term change. 3. Help client recognize and manage triggers to return to use. 4. Affirm client's commitment to ongoing change. 5. Support problem solving of barriers encountered in the change process. **Skills** 1. Use OARS 2. Revisit Phase 1 or 2 skills as appropriate. 3. Avoid traps and hazards.

POTENTIAL TREATMENT GOALS		
1. If client relapses, identify areas for addressing and preventing future relapse. 2. Client will reevaluate recovery environment in regard to long-term recovery; this could include prosocial coping skills, employment situations, anger-management needs, and family support. 3. Update new goals for quality living. 4. Client will maintain goals set for self that support important lifestyle changes. 5. Client will develop coping skills and share these with others in Twelve Step or other support groups. 6. Client will build self-efficacy through focusing on successes made toward his recovery.		

As some of you may know, the view presented here is not typical of the way MI and SOC concepts are usually presented. MI and SOC were developed separately in the research world and continue to be refined through exhaustive research as separate though compatible paradigms. We recognize, appreciate, and support these efforts. In the world of clinical practice, however, the complexities clients face and the issues they bring to counseling require that effective programs and practitioners address these issues and provide the best possible care. In the authors' experiences, MI and SOC work well together in providing authentic and genuine care for clients who need or seek to change their behavior. For these reasons, we have offered a blending of MI and SOC to assist counselors in their practice with their clients. The preceding grids, integrating Motivational Interviewing with Stages and Processes of Change, will assist counselors to do the following:

1. Remember the research findings, which are found to be true regarding successful behavior change.

2. Encourage focus on the client to ensure that the client's desires, motivations, and confidences for change are reinforced.

3. Recognize that change can be reinforced through the counseling process by attending to the place clients are at in the process of change coupled with specific skills that move them toward change.

4. Create a framework for how to look at the counseling process.

5. Identify skills and strategies that work well with clients at certain stages in the change process.

6. Create an easy reference to use in their daily work with clients.

7. Remind them to put into action what will work best for clients.

There is, of course, much more to the concepts, beliefs, and approaches to Motivational Interviewing and Stages of Change. We encourage the reader to learn more by reading the works identified in the bibliography section. We move next to a presentation of how MI and SOC can work together in practical application.

■ ■ ■

OPENING THE DOOR TO CHANGE

*The real voyage of discovery lies not in seeking
new landscapes, but in having new eyes.*

— MARCEL PROUST

This chapter focuses on the precontemplation and contemplation stages of change, although some of the activities will be appropriate for the preparation stage as well. During these two stages, clients need to build motivation and increase their confidence for change. Definitions of these stages, relevant processes of change, and a list of strategies for counselors are contained in the table on page 36.

In the precontemplation stage, clients may be fending off attempts by others to convince them to change their drug use, may be in denial, or may be innocently unaware that their use is problematic. Generally, clients need to increase their factual knowledge and raise their awareness about a need for change. The counselor's goal in this stage is to identify clients' defenses and raise their awareness of their problematic behavior.

As clients move into the contemplation stage, they begin to consider the possibility that changing their behavior might be a good idea. They are unsure about whether to change or stay the same. Their ambivalence is prominent and will be a factor throughout most of the remaining stages of change. During the contemplation stage, the counselor's goal is to encourage clients to make a decision for change.

Appropriate Motivational Strategies for Precontemplation and Contemplation Stages of Change[1]

CLIENT'S STAGE OF CHANGE	MOTIVATIONAL STRATEGIES FOR COUNSELORS

PRECONTEMPLATION STAGE
 	
The client is not yet considering change or is unwilling or unable to change.
 	
Process of Change
 	
Consciousness Raising
Increasing awareness about the effects of client's substance use on himself and others
 	
Emotional Arousal
Emotional experiences that the client has leading to thinking about changing his substance use
	• Establish rapport, ask permission, and build trust.
	• Raise doubts or concerns in the client about substance-using patterns by
	  – exploring the meaning of events that brought the client to treatment or the results of previous treatments
	  – eliciting the client's perceptions of the problem
	  – offering factual information about the risks of substance use
	  – providing personalized feedback about assessment findings
	  – exploring the pros and cons of substance use
	  – helping a significant other intervene
	  – examining discrepancies between the client's and others' perceptions of the problem behavior
	  – expressing concern and keeping the door open

CONTEMPLATION STAGE
 	
The client acknowledges concerns and considers the possibility of change but is ambivalent and uncertain.
 	
Process of Change
 	
Environmental Reevaluation
Looking at and reacting to the client's external and internal experiences as they relate to changing substance use
 	
Social Liberation
Identifying and utilizing the supports society offers to change substance use
 	
Helping Relationships
Establishing supportive relationships while changing client's behavior related to substance use
	• Normalize ambivalence.
	• Help the client "tip the decisional balance scales" toward change by
	  – eliciting and weighing the pros and cons of substance use and change
	  – changing extrinsic to intrinsic motivation
	  – examining the client's personal values in relation to change
	  – emphasizing the client's free choice, responsibility, and self-efficacy for change
	  – eliciting self-motivational statements of intent and commitment from the client
	  – eliciting ideas regarding the client's perceived self-efficacy and expectations regarding treatment
	  – summarizing self-motivational statements

It is important to keep in mind that most clients entering treatment programs are not committed to doing anything about their drug use or have mixed feelings about changing. This is normal and predictable during the early part of the change process. To expect clients to behave otherwise is unrealistic and can often solidify their decision not to change.

All too often, two key issues in the early stages of change—lack of interest in or lack of willingness to change, and ambivalence about changing drug-using behavior—have been neglected, ignored, or addressed ineffectively in traditional treatment settings. Research reported earlier has revealed that attending to these issues and developing appropriate interventions can result in improved client retention, engagement, and treatment outcomes. MI and SOC approaches have been shown to result in these sort of treatment enhancements and therefore can be of great assistance to clients as they work toward eliminating their destructive drug use. In addition to being beneficial for clients, improvements of this nature can increase satisfaction for counselors as they work with clients they have not been so successful with in the past. Counselors who have used this approach report a sense of relief, often stating that being more client-centered and attending to the change process allows them to truly focus on their clients. The sense of responsibility for change shifts from counselor to client, supporting an environment that enhances respect and dignity for clients, as well as freedom for counselors to use their skills and talents to assist clients to move toward change at their own pace and within their own time frame.

The six activities contained in this chapter are

- Identifying the Client's Stage of Change
- Establish Rapport
- Readiness for Change
- Decisional Balance
- Collaborating for Choices
- Individualizing Feedback

Each activity is presented with a chart showing the stages of change in which it is most helpful, the relevant processes of change, the primary MI skills and strategies that are effective in completing the activity, and the settings in which the activity would most likely be useful.

Activity 1:

Identifying the Client's Stage of Change

SOC:	All
POC:	Consciousness raising, self-reevaluation, social liberation
MI Strategies:	Maintain MI style; build rapport and trust; with permission, explore and normalize ambivalence; remain client-centered; reduce resistance as needed
MI Skills:	Monitor tone of voice, gestures; use OARS; elicit change talk; avoid traps
Appropriate for:	Individual session; can be modified for group session

Purpose

This activity is an interactive exercise designed to assist the counselor and client in determining the client's current stage of change. It is also designed to evaluate the client's progress through change by highlighting in client-friendly language the experiential and behavioral processes of change.

Introduction

This first activity will help ensure that the counselor has a frame of reference for working with clients and will be able to use the suggested strategies throughout the various stages of change. The counselor will need to have a good understanding of the Transtheoretical Model of Change and the processes of change as well as consider blending the MI skills and strategies into the process of the exercises.

Before beginning this activity, it may be helpful to review the basic information in chapter 2 of the book *Changing for Good* by Prochaska, Norcross, and DiClemente (see bibliography) and material located at the Cancer Prevention Research Center (CPRC) at the University of Rhode Island Web page (see resources).

Located at the end of activity 1 are three handouts. Two are for clients (Stages of Change, Client Stage of Change), and one is for counselors (Counselor Stage of Change Key). All three are written in an easy-to-understand manner. Please note that there is an additional version of the Client Stage of Change handout. It is designed for use with adolescents. In addition, we strongly encourage you to translate the handout for your non-English-speaking clients. The Counselor Stage of Change Key works with both adult and youth groups.

Activity Steps

1. Prepare for the session by making a copy of the following handouts:

   a. Stages of Change

   b. Client Stage of Change (also Youth Stage of Change)

   c. Counselor Stage of Change Key

2. Give the Stages of Change handout to the client and review the stages of change using the information on the sheet. After the material has been reviewed, ask the client to report his thoughts and feelings regarding the information, using MI Phase 1 OARS. For example:

   Counselor: Now that I presented the stages of change to you, I am wondering what reactions you might be having regarding the information (i.e., your referral for treatment, your alcohol use, your feelings about being mandated, etc.) as it applies to you.

   Client: Well, I am not sure. I may be in between some of the stages.

   Counselor: The information seems to make sense to you, but it is hard to place yourself in a specific stage of change.

   Client: Yeah! Sometimes I think I'm in this second stage (client points to the contemplation stage on the handout) and sometimes I think I am like this (points to the precontemplation stage). I don't know.

   Counselor: Sounds like it might be a bit confusing right now. It is very normal, however, for you to feel like you are in two different places at the same time. Let's take a closer look at this. Would you be willing to work with me to complete this next handout (Client Stage of Change)?

3. Describe the processes of change and how they are related to the stages of change, using the handout as a visual to track with the client and using language that will make sense to the client. (Note: The Client Stage of Change handout on page 45 has simplified the processes of change language so the client can more easily understand the concepts presented.)

Duplicating this page is illegal. Do not copy this material without written permission from the publisher.

39

4. To help the client understand the processes of change, ask him to think of a change he has made in the past. Ask him to point to the processes he may have used when he was making that change. Process using MI Phase 1 skills and strategies.

5. Ask the client to think about the current change facing him now.

6. Use OARS to process the information with the client. Remember the importance of staying client-focused and listening well.

7. Ask the client to circle the processes of change as they relate to his current circumstances.

8. After the client circles his responses on the handout, review his responses with him.

   Note: Use the Counselor Stage of Change Key as a reminder of key definitions of the processes of change and to help you assist the client in determining his stage of change. The key is designed so that the common terms are paired with the corresponding research terminology and the stage of change that those processes typically represent.

9. Remind the client that the processes of change are related to the stages of change. For example, if the client has circled processes of change primarily in the E (experience) section of the handout, explain to the client that he is most likely in the earlier stages of change. If the client circles mostly processes in the B (behavior) section of the handout, explain that he is most likely in the middle to later stages of change. If the numbers of processes circled in both are equal, the client is likely to be in the preparation stage, moving toward action.

10. Refer the client back to the Stages of Change handout and explore those stages that match the circled processes of change.

11. Once the stage of change is determined, you are free to explore the client's perception, goals, and ideas throughout the counseling process, while continuing to build rapport, trust, and a safe environment for exploration.

Activity Application

1. Spend some time with clients highlighting what they may want to change as well as how the information reflects changes they have made in the past.

2. Certain MI skills can be applied to this process. For example, if, at the end of this activity, a client's stage of change is determined to be precontemplation, you can ask the following open-ended questions:

   "What would have to happen to you for you to consider making a change?

   "How could I help you reach your goals today?"

   "What would you be interested in knowing about _____?"

   Other open-ended questions can be used for different stages of change as you get acquainted with clients and their needs.

3. Using OARS and eliciting change talk are good initial skills and strategies to use in this activity.

4. Stay on track with clients' needs and avoid the Phase 1 traps, such as premature focus or asking too many questions and forgetting to reflect often.

5. In SOC theory, an approximate amount of time is required for people to progress through each stage, so there is a temporal component to stage identification. For example, the University of Rhode Island Change Assessment Scale (URICA), a researched-based instrument designed to measure an individual's stage of change, allows increments of six months between each of the earlier stages. Although it is important to attend to temporal issues, what is more important in these earlier stages of change is to stay with clients while they fluctuate in and out of various stages. Sometimes clients will waffle between stages frequently. Identifying the process of change is more useful to clients than labeling them as being in a stage.

6. This activity can be repeated throughout the counseling process to show progress or to identify where clients may be stuck.

7. Remember that clients can fluctuate quickly and appear to be in more than one stage of change. Attend to this process by assessing readiness regularly. Switch strategies according to where clients are at the time.

Stages of Change

Following are brief descriptions of how many people move through major changes in their lives. Each stage of change is defined in friendly terms along with the actual terms researchers use to determine an individual's current place in the process of change.

1. Precontemplation Stage of Change

➤ NOTHING NEEDS TO CHANGE.

What you may hear during this stage of change:

"My life is fine. There are no problems with my substance use or anything else."

"At times, I have noticed that things get out of hand for me, and others have commented about my use. However, I have no concerns right now and see no need to change."

2. Contemplation Stage of Change

➤ I AM THINKING ABOUT CHANGING.

What you may hear during this stage of change:

"Part of me thinks I would like to see if I could cut down on using, and another part of me thinks I'm okay with what I am doing now."

"When others tell me I need to change, I find myself telling them why I cannot or that now is not a good time. Sometimes I think I should change, but other times I don't know."

continued on other side

3. Preparation Stage of Change

➤ I AM DECIDING ON HOW TO CHANGE.

What you may hear during this stage of change:

> *"I have made the decision to change, but I am not sure how to go about it."*

> *"I know I can change, but I may need some more information on the best way to accomplish my goals."*

4. Action Stage of Change

➤ I'M MAKING THE CHANGES I WANT.

What you may hear during this stage of change:

> *"I am making changes and having success with reaching my goals."*

> *"Even though the changes I am making can be challenging at times, I have been able to adjust and feel more and more confident that I can get through this process."*

5. Maintenance Stage of Change

➤ I MADE THE CHANGES I WANT; IT IS TIME TO STICK WITH THEM AND MAINTAIN MY GAINS.

What you may hear during this stage of change:

> *"I am committed to maintaining the changes I have made."*

> *"Even though I had a slip or relapse, I plan to keep working on maintaining the changes I have made."*

Experiences I have that might create change:

Self-reflection

Becoming aware

EXPERIENCES

Societal support for change

Sensational emotions

Influence of others

Behaviors that are helping me maintain the changes I have made
or am attempting:

Supportive influences

Choosing something new

Creating a plan

BEHAVIORS

Celebrating improvements

Managing my change

Counselor Stage of Change Key

EXPERIENCES the client has that create change: _____

Self-reflection

Contemplation, preparation

Assessing values against your
feelings and behavior *(self-reevaluation)*

Sensational emotions

Contemplation

Strong negative emotions that create a
need for change *(emotional arousal)*

Becoming aware

Precontemplation

(consciousness raising)

Societal support for change

All stages

Societal procedures that make change easier
(social liberation)

Influence of others

Precontemplation, contemplation

How your behavior affects others
(environmental reevaluation)

BEHAVIORS that are helping the client maintain change: _____

Supportive influences

Most stages

(helping relationships)

Choosing something new

Preparation

What to do instead of using
(counterconditioning)

Managing my change

Preparation

Having hope for success in the future
(self-liberation)

Celebrating improvements

Action

Reward progress toward change
(reinforcement management)

Creating a plan

Maintenance

Managing triggers, situations, etc.
(stimulus control)

Duplicating this page for personal or group use is permissible.

47

Experiences I have that might create change:

Looking at myself

Intense feelings

EXPERIENCES

Becoming aware

Community support for change

Influence of others

Behaviors that are helping me maintain the changes I have made or am attempting:

Supportive of others

Choosing something new

Celebrating improvements

BEHAVIORS

Monitoring how I do

Activity 2:

Establish Rapport

SOC:	Precontemplation
POC:	Consciousness raising
MI Strategies:	Maintain MI style; build rapport and trust; engage client; remain client-centered; monitor resistance
MI Skills:	Monitor tone of voice, gestures; use OARS; elicit client concerns; avoid Phase 1 traps
Appropriate for:	Individual session

Purpose

This activity is designed to create an environment that permits exploration of behavior change by (1) establishing client-counselor rapport, (2) asking permission to explore change, and (3) building a trusting relationship in which collaboration can occur.

Introduction

One of the earliest and most important aspects of counseling is establishing a relationship with clients. From the very first contact, counselors work to create a collaborative, trusting environment in which clients are encouraged to become active partners with their counselors in the treatment process. This activity illustrates an approach that allows counselors to be client-centered.

Since the first contact with clients is frequently an assessment, the activity is presented as an assessment session. While this activity is designed for the client in precontemplation, it can be used with clients at any stage of change.

The activity is presented in three parts: opening the session, counselor/ agency agenda (for example, gathering data), and closing the session.

Activity Steps

PART 1: OPENING THE SESSION

1. Greet the client.

   a. Use her name and establish eye contact if culturally appropriate.

   b. Offer to shake hands.

   c. Ask a question designed to put her at ease, such as "Did you have difficulty getting here today?" or "How was the drive?"

   d. Offer choice of seating.

2. Start the session with an open-ended question, such as "What brings you here today?" or "How can I be of assistance?"

3. Reflect her responses and ask for clarification throughout the interview.

4. Spend ten to fifteen minutes in this type of exploration.

5. Summarize the discussion thus far.

6. Request permission to change the pace to an assessment style.

7. Describe the assessment process, being sure to address confidentiality issues.

8. Ask if she has any questions about what will happen.

9. Ask if there is something specific she would like to get from the appointment.

PART 2: COUNSELOR/AGENCY AGENDA

1. Remind the client that now you will have to gather some information, so you will need to ask questions during this part of the process.

2. Ask permission to continue.

3. Proceed using your organization's assessment forms.

PART 3: CLOSING THE SESSION

1. Summarize what the client said in the session.

2. Based on this sumary, offer your initial impressions about her situation. Take care to avoid labeling.

3. If resistance arises, remember to reflect, empower, and offer choices.

4. Provide options for the next steps and ask the client how she wants to proceed.

Activity Application

1. The initial greeting of clients in this activity sets the environment for the interview, letting them know you are interested in them and their experiences, and that they will have some choices in this situation. Asking what they want from the interview continues to engage them in the process, indicating that they are not powerless and left to the program's or counselor's agenda only. Offering choices or options enhances the sense that this is a collaborative process. Often, mandated clients will verbalize issues *they* want to address, which may or may not meet the agenda of the program.

2. When you tell clients that you have to gather data and will be asking specific questions, you are preparing them for what's to come. Asking their permission emphasizes the MI style, which is important, especially early on. Should clients deny permission to continue, your role is to accept that decision and help them understand the consequences of their choice. A nonjudgmental, informative manner conveys your understanding that they are in charge. It is up to them to make the right decisions.

3. Closing the session by summarizing what clients have said keeps the focus on them. Again, offering information about what options are available and asking them to choose their options continues the engagement process and builds the collaborative element of the relationship. Clients often express their interest in your thoughts and impressions. In responding to their requests for information, avoid the Phase 1 traps, such as acting like an expert, labeling, or blaming. This is especially important with mandated clients who frequently feel that they have no choices since they have been made to come to this session. Remember to use your skills at managing resistance, keeping the clients engaged. Improving the possibility of getting their needs met is more likely to meet the goals of the mandate while decreasing the probability of negative consequences, such as further criminal activity, work or school problems, or increasing severity of their symptoms.

Activity 3:

Readiness for Change

SOC:	Precontemplation, contemplation (*Note:* Can be used for all stages as needed)
POC:	Consciousness raising, self-reevaluation, social liberation, emotional arousal, self-liberation, environmental reevaluation
MI Strategies:	Maintain MI style; explore motivation and confidence; identify discrepancies; explore goals and values; identify client strengths; monitor resistance; normalize ambivalence; build self-efficacy; engage client, client-centered
MI Skills:	Monitor tone of voice, gestures; use OARS; elicit change talk; avoid traps
Appropriate for:	Individual session; can be modified for group or family session

Purpose

This exercise allows counselors to assess clients' readiness and motivation for change.

Introduction

This is a scaling activity that is particularly helpful in the earlier stages of change, although it can be useful throughout most stages. Maintaining a client-centered approach is central, so counselors need to be tuned in to a client's readiness to change. This awareness will help counselors maintain a collaborative approach with their clients. Counselors must avoid the temptation to lead the way or push clients beyond their point of preparedness. Experience tells us that losing touch with where clients are often results in increased resistance rather than facilitated movement. The following activity steps are presented in a script format for ease of use. The script is designed to assess a client's readiness for change regarding a specific behavioral issue such as substance abuse.

Activity Steps

1. Counselor and client agree to the behavioral indicator, for example, substance abuse.

2. Counselor asks: "On a scale of one to ten, with one being 'I'm not willing to change my substance use' and ten being 'I will do anything that I need to in order to change my substance use,' how would you rate your willingness to address your substance-using behavior?"

3. Client responds with a number. Counselor repeats the number.

4. Counselor asks: "Why did you choose that number?" Client responds.

5. Counselor asks: "Is there anything else? Tell me more about that." After client responds, counselor reflects, empathizes, and elicits.

6. Counselor asks: "Tell me, why didn't you pick a lower number?" After client responds, counselor reflects, empathizes, and elicits.

7. Counselor asks: "Is there anything more? What else?" After client responds, counselor reflects, empathizes, and elicits.

8. Counselor asks: "What would it take for you to go to a _____ (state a number two to three numbers higher than the client's first one)?" After client responds, counselor reflects, empathizes, and elicits.

9. Counselor summarizes and asks: "Did I miss anything? Where does that leave you now?"

Activity Application

The activity helps you attend to several early-stage issues and use key skills.

1. Reflective listening is essential to staying client-centered.

   Clients will often surprise themselves with how motivated they actually are to make changes. Reflective listening may give you valuable information about your clients' level of willingness to make a specific change they have been considering.

2. Having clients scale their willingness to change a particular behavior helps them to recognize that they have *some* willingness, even if they rate it as low as a two. Repeating the number chosen assures clients that you have heard them.

3. Depending on clients' level of concern or mixed feelings about change, you can respond appropriately. You can acknowledge that some clients are not yet ready to change, and then use strategies such as exploring the pros and cons of change. For those clients prepared to move forward, you can move on to other strategies, such as identifying barriers to change and ways to address them.

4. Asking for more information indicates that you are interested and prompts clients to explore how they feel about change and the impact it might have on their lives.

5. Again, asking for further information is an indication that you are interested and also helps clients look more deeply into their attitudes about change.

Activity 4:

Decisional Balance

SOC:	Contemplation
POC:	Self-reevaluation, consciousness raising, self-liberation, environmental reevaluation, counterconditioning
MI Strategies:	Maintain MI style; develop discrepancies; explore goals and values; elicit change; identify client reasons, abilities, need, and desire for change; explore ambivalence; empower client; remain client-centered; monitor resistance
MI Skills:	Monitor tone of voice, gestures; use OARS; elicit change talk; if appropriate, use transitional summary and/or key questions; avoid traps
Appropriate for:	Individual session; can be modified for group or family session

Purpose

This activity helps clients resolve their discrepancies about changing a particular behavior by exploring the pros and cons of that behavior. A transitional summary, followed by key open-ended questions, is intended to help clients proceed to the next step in their process of change.

Introduction

The decisional balance activity is begun after the counselor has established a relationship with the client, which sets the stage for more detailed exploration and potential discrepancy building. This activity gives the client an opportunity to explore in detail the positive and negative aspects of both continuing and stopping an identified behavior. It is important to end the exploration with the positive aspects of change so as to leave the client with a mind-set that favors change.

The following steps for the transitional summary and key questions are clearly labeled for use when appropriate. A transitional summary is one that brings together elements of the interaction to identify or indicate a change, such as the end of a session or the movement from the contemplation stage to the preparation stage. A summary may help when shifting from Phase 1, Building Motivation for Change, to Phase 2, Strengthening Commitment to Change.

Activity Steps

1. Explain the activity and show the client the Decisional Balance Worksheet[2] on page 60, or outline the columns on a chalkboard, piece of newsprint, or flip chart.

2. Ask permission to explore the client's reasons for both continuing and stopping use of a given substance.

3. Begin by exploring first the pros and then the cons of continuing use. *Summarize, elicit change talk.*

4. Next, explore first the cons and then the pros of stopping use. *Summarize, elicit change talk.*

5. Offer information and advice as requested or needed.

Optional Steps: Completing a Transitional Summary/Key Questions

1. Summarize the client's perception of the problem.

2. Identify the client's verbalized reasons to change.

3. Point out that the client is less ambivalent about taking the next step toward change.

4. Include the client's statements about what positive results she wants from changing.

Activity Application

1. It is important for counselors to remain neutral and patient during this activity. The use of mini summaries throughout the process helps keep clients on track. The subtle, directive nature of MI becomes apparent here as counselors choose those items to emphasize in summarizing.

2. Transitional summaries are strategically used to highlight client change talk. What the practitioner decides to highlight are the client statements that emphasize concerns, importance, hope, and intentions toward change. Inherent in using a transitional summary is the expression of hope for the client to achieve the change or changes desired.

3. This activity can be used throughout the earlier stages of change, when clients are still unsure about changing and may feel stuck, or when they lack motivation or confidence to move toward change. It can be repeated as a way to periodically measure clients' movement away from or toward change.

Decisional Balance Worksheet

Name: _____

Date: _____

PROS AND CONS

CONTINUING BEHAVIOR		STOPPING BEHAVIOR	
PROS (Benefits)	**CONS** (Costs)	**CONS** (Costs)	**PROS** (Benefits)

The above worksheet is adapted from *Motivational Interviewing: Preparing People for Change*, 2d ed., by William R. Miller and Stephen Rollnick (Guilford Press 2002) 16, with permission.

Activity 5:

Collaborating for Choices

SOC:	Contemplation, preparation (can be used in all stages of change)
POC:	Stimulus control, self-evaluation, self-liberation, emotional arousal, counterconditioning
MI Strategies:	Maintain MI style; explore goals and values; identify client strengths; empower client; process ambivalence; negotiate a change plan
MI Skills:	Monitor tone of voice, gestures; use OARS; elicit change talk; avoid traps
Appropriate for:	Individual session; can be modified for group or family session

Purpose

This activity identifies client choices and supports responsible decision making.

Introduction

This is a collaborative activity in which the counselor both models for and works with clients to explore the possible options related to a given behavior, such as going to treatment, attending Twelve Step meetings, abstaining from use, or making a change of some sort. It helps clients in the early stages of change clarify the realistic costs and benefits of their behavior and thereby encourages their movement toward making a decision to change. The activity also gives counselors the opportunity to support clients in making choices and accepting responsibility for their actions. It is also useful in later stages as clients solidify their decisions and start planning to make the changes they have chosen.

Activity Steps

1. Introduce the topic of the session, such as deciding what the client will choose to work on in treatment. (Note: See the example on page 62.)

2. Draw up to five circles on a piece of paper or chalkboard. Each circle represents an option the client can choose.

3. Introduce a choice by naming it and explaining that it is a choice.

4. Then, write the choice in one of the circles.

5. Leave one or two circles blank and ask the client to fill them in.

6. Repeat steps 2 through 6 until the client identifies an option she is willing to try.

7. Next, ask the client to name both the positive and negative consequences of the choice.

8. List all of the consequences.

9. With the client, identify and list barriers that might arise.

10. Together, explore barriers and list solutions as appropriate.

Example

An illustration may help clarify the steps of this activity. In the example below, the client's issue is deciding about use. First, the counselor draws circles, as shown. The counselor then fills in realistic options, leaving one circle blank for the client to fill in.

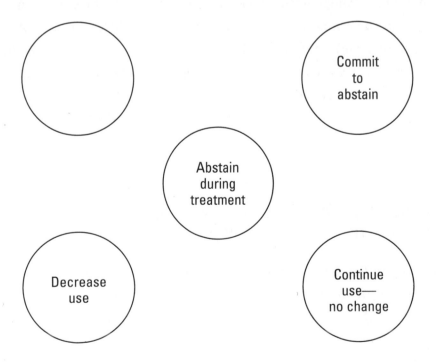

The client chooses to work on decreasing use.

The counselor draws the columns as shown below and, together with the client, fills them in.

Consequences

POSITIVE	NEGATIVE
1. I won't have to give up my use totally.	1. I may not succeed.
2. I'll feel more in control.	2. My friends won't support me.
3. I'll keep my friends.	3. People close to me will be angry that I don't stop altogether.
4. I can still relax and feel less anxious.	4. I will get depressed.

BARRIERS	SOLUTIONS
1. This won't satisfy my mandate.	1. I can't win—I have to comply with my mandate.
2. I'll have problems at home.	2. I will demonstrate the behavior expected (being on time, reduced conflicts, etc.).

Activity Application

You should strive to remain objective and neutral throughout this process and elicit the client's perspective in order to empower her. Some of the important and subtle steps to attend to include the following:

1. Engage the client by making the activity visual, drawing circles as illustrated on page 62.

2. Keep focused on the client's nonverbal and verbal responses as you involve her in the activity.

3. Remind the client that she is making these choices for herself, not for others to judge.

4. Help the client to recognize and understand the connection between making choices and taking responsibility for those choices. Be sure she is mindful of the potential consequences and is willing to accept them.

5. Tie her choices to what is important to her and what she values.

6. Frame barriers as obstacles to solve rather than reasons to stay stuck.

7. Remind her that she is the expert on her own life.

8. Remain nonjudgmental and supportive, and help problem solve as needed.

9. Make sure the client knows you will be available if she wants to reevaluate or reconsider her choice.

10. Be aware that as the client explores barriers to her choice, she may change her mind about the option she wants to work on.

Activity 6:

Individualizing Feedback

SOC:	Contemplation, preparation (can be used in all stages of change)
POC:	Stimulus control, self-evaluation, self-liberation, emotional arousal, counterconditioning
MI Strategies:	Maintain MI style; explore goals and values; identify client strengths; empower client; process ambivalence; negotiate a change plan
MI Skills:	Monitor tone of voice, gestures; use OARS; elicit change talk; avoid traps
Appropriate for:	Individual session; can be modified for group or family session

Purpose

To provide factual information regarding the use of relevant substance or substances in order to raise clients' awareness about the role of substances in their lives.

Introduction

This activity is one simple way of applying the key concept of individualizing treatment. Counselors compare clients' information with demographic data in order to help clients see the disparity between their substance use and the substance use of the larger population. It is important for counselors to have data for comparison that most closely reflects the demographics of the client they are meeting with. (A resource for this demographic data for each state is available on the SAMHSA Web site. See the resources section for this Web site.)

The following activity steps are based on information gathered from a client assessment process.

Activity Steps

1. Choose one fact from the client's assessment that can be compared to demographic information. (For example, the number of drinks per week.)

2. Present the client's information in comparison to demographic information.

3. Ask the client what he thinks about the information provided.

4. Use OARS to process his reaction.

5. If resistance arises, roll with resistance, reflecting the client's concerns and reactions.

6. Continue to compare the client assessment information with the demographic information and process the client's reaction.

Activity Application

1. Choosing one fact from the client's assessment and asking the client to compare it with the demographic data helps raise the client's doubts about his interpretation of his behavior as normal or ordinary. He is likely to become uncomfortable when confronted with the disparity and may respond with resistance. It is important that you stay focused on him and reflect his emotions, reactions, and concerns.

2. The directive nature of this style becomes apparent in the following exchange between a female counselor and a male client. Notice how the counselor lets the client know she is attentive to his concerns, avoids engaging in arguments with him, and uses an open-ended question to change the subject to one of her choosing, namely exploring how to proceed in the treatment program.

> *Counselor:* What are your thoughts about your blood alcohol content (BAC) and how it compares with the legal BAC limits?
>
> *Client:* Well, I think the limit is way too high. All of my friends use, and they don't have problems. I think the law needs to be changed.
>
> *Counselor:* It seems that the legal limits are unrealistic to you.
>
> *Client:* I don't drink more than my friends. We work, have families, and live our lives. It just is not fair. I know people who use a hell of a lot more than I do.

Counselor: It is unfair and unjust to you.

Client: Absolutely!

(At this point the counselor chooses a directive strategy. Asking a specifically chosen open-ended question changes the focus of the interaction.)

Counselor: Given that you feel the information you are hearing is unfair or should not be applied to you, and that you are mandated to come here, how would you like the program to work with you around the requirements of your mandate?

Client: Well, I don't know. I don't want to go to jail or lose my job over this. Can you tell them I don't have a problem?

Counselor: Whether or not you have a problem with alcohol is something for you to decide. What I can do is give you more information for your consideration, allow you some time to think about what that means to you, and, through the program, expose you to others in situations similar to yours. Would that be something you would like to pursue?

3. This interaction leaves the client feeling in control, but he is now in control of a subject chosen by the counselor.

◼

Using these activities with your clients will allow you to practice MI skills and strategies and develop a level of comfort in using them. The activities themselves enhance your efforts to engage and retain your clients as well as create a counseling relationship that is supportive and sensitive to clients' needs and readiness to change, and in which clients feel comfortable sharing their stories with you.

In the next chapter, we build on these activities and move our focus to other aspects of clients' struggles and concerns, including the conflicting feelings they have about changing behaviors that are both problematic and enjoyable.

Duplicating this page is illegal. Do not copy this material without written permission from the publisher.

67

PLANNING FOR AND IMPLEMENTING CHANGE

The first step toward change is acceptance.
Change is not something you do; it's something you allow.

— WILL GARCIA

Once clients have made the decision to change, they move along the stages of change toward the preparation and action stages. As they begin exploring ways to plan for and implement change, MI Phase 2 strategies—assessing readiness, transitional summary and key questions, offering information and advice, and negotiating change plans—come into play. These strategies are described in chapter 2.

Formulating a realistic plan for change is the first challenge. In the preparation stage, clients have made the decision to change but often have little or no idea of how to go about making change happen. The counselor's job at this time is to help clients prepare for change by assisting and supporting them through a planning process. It is crucial for the counselor to acknowledge and normalize any feelings of incompetence clients may have while instilling in them hope for their future and confidence in their ability to succeed. Viable, useful plans must include well-defined goals and concrete, measurable behaviors geared to meet those goals. Clients need help to think out and state clearly their reasons for altering their behavior and to identify the barriers they are likely to encounter. In addition, they need support for their new course of action from others in their environment. Helping clients recognize existing resources and explore options for support and encouragement is a significant part of creating an effective plan.

The next challenge, the central element of the action stage, is to implement the plan for change. As clients begin to act on their change plans, they need feedback about what is working, what needs modification, and what should be

Duplicating this page is illegal. Do not copy this material without written permission from the publisher.

69

eliminated altogether. They also need encouragement to continue pursuing their goals. Therefore, the counselor's objective here is to monitor clients' progress and assist them as they implement their change plans.

Counselors frequently find the preparation and action stages satisfying and productive for their clients and, as a result, fulfilling for themselves. Clients' motivation is usually strong, and their confidence is growing. Their self-efficacy is rising and change sometimes occurs rapidly. Multiple-drug-using clients who are succeeding in changing their use of one drug may verbalize concerns about their use of other drugs and may ask for help reducing or eliminating such use.

At this stage, counselors may slip into thinking that their job is done. They may think that all they need to do is relax and enjoy the positive strides their clients are making. While that may be the case with some clients, it is not true of everyone. It is essential for counselors to remain prepared for the ongoing possibility of ambivalence and to be mindful of the fragile nature of many clients' commitments to change. This is a time when clients often vacillate and test their commitments. Staying client-centered and reinforcing clients' confidence in their ability to change (self-efficacy) is crucial during this period. As you monitor progress, it is important to avoid the MI Phase 2 traps of over-prescription, underestimating ambivalence, and giving insufficient direction. These traps can inadvertently slow or frustrate clients' progress or even result in their regression.

The chart on the next page lists useful strategies for counselors to pursue with clients who are in the preparation and action stages of change and the processes of change important at each stage. The activities that follow are options for addressing some of these strategies.

Appropriate Motivational Strategies for Preparation and Action Stages of Change[1]

CLIENT'S STAGE OF CHANGE	MOTIVATIONAL STRATEGIES FOR COUNSELORS
PREPARATION STAGE The client is committed to and planning to make a change in the near future but is still considering what to do. **Process of Change** *Self-Liberation* Experiencing hope and confidence in one's ability to address substance abuse issues *Social Liberation* Identifying and utilizing the supports society offers to change substance use *Helping Relationships* Establishing supportive relationships while changing behavior related to substance use	• Clarify the client's own goals and strategies for change. • Offer a menu of options for change or treatment. • With permission, offer expertise and advice. • Negotiate a change—or treatment—plan and behavior contract. • Consider and lower barriers to change. • Help the client enlist social support. • Explore treatment expectancies and the client's role. • Elicit from the client what has worked in the past, either for him or others whom he knows. • Assist the client to negotiate finances, child care, work, transportation, or other potential barriers. • Have the client publicly announce plans to change.
ACTION STAGE The client is actively taking steps to change but has not yet reached a stable state. **Process of Change** *Counterconditioning* Creating options besides continued substance use *Reinforcement Management* Celebrating self for changing *Stimulus Control* Managing urges and triggers to use substances *Social Liberation* Identifying and utilizing the supports society offers to change substance use	• Engage the client in treatment and reinforce the importance of remaining in recovery. • Support a realistic view of change through small steps. • Acknowledge difficulties for the client in early stages of change. • Help the client identify high-risk situations through a functional analysis and develop appropriate coping strategies to overcome these. • Assist the client in finding new reinforcers of positive change. • Help the client assess support strength.

Four activities are included in this chapter:

- Goals for Change
- Developing a Change Plan
- Ready, Willing, and Able
- Building Hope for Change

These activities can help you determine clients' readiness for change, assist them to build hope that change is possible, facilitate working together on the change-planning process, and support clients in finding ways to reduce barriers to implementing changes. Each activity is preceded by a chart showing the stages of change in which it is most helpful, the relevant processes of change, the primary MI skills and strategies that are effective in completing the activity, and the settings in which the activity would most likely be useful.

Activity 1:

Goals for Change

SOC:	Preparation, contemplation
POC:	Consciousness raising, self-reevaluation, environmental reevaluation, social liberation
MI Strategies:	Maintain MI style; elicit change talk; explore goals and values; monitor client resistance; reinforce change talk
MI Skills:	Monitor tone of voice, gestures; use OARS; avoid traps
Appropriate for:	Individual session; can be modified for group or family session

Purpose

This activity will enable clients to identify a change they wish to make in a specific area and prepare them to make a change plan for that area.

Introduction

As clients reach the preparation stage of change, they often find that there are many changes they wish to make. You can help them increase their chances of success by working with them to prioritize changes based on their values. This activity is often used together with Activity 2: Developing a Change Plan.

Activity Steps

1. Present a list of values (see sample list on page 74).

2. Ask, "On this list of values, which two are most important to you in your life right now?"

   Explore client's preferences and reasons for them.

   Reflect, empathize, elicit.

3. Say, "Tell me why they are important to you now."

   Reflect, empathize, elicit.

4. Present a list of life areas (see sample list on page 74).

5. Say, "Keeping in mind what you have said about what values are important to you, choose two of these areas that are the most important in your life right now."

Reflect, empathize, elicit.

6. Ask, "What is important about these life areas and how do they link with your values?"

Reflect, empathize, elicit.

7. Ask, "Which area would you like to work on making a change plan for?"

8. Proceed to activity 2, Developing a Change Plan, now or next session, depending on the amount of time available.

EXAMPLE
Lists of values and life areas

VALUES	LIFE AREAS
Honesty	Family/friends
Hard work	Emotional
Fairness	Work/school
Pleasure	Health
Education	Legal
Money	Spiritual
Belonging	
Adventure	
Sex	

Activity Application

1. Clients are more likely to be successful in making changes when the changes are ones they have chosen rather than ones other people identify as being "good for them."

2. Key counselor behaviors involve staying neutral, following the client's lead, and offering suggestions only after receiving the client's permission.

3. It is also important to remind clients that it is possible to rethink decisions and change one's mind. To do so is normal.

4. Maintain a nonjudgmental atmosphere, so clients know there are no right or wrong responses or answers.

Activity 2:

Developing a Change Plan

SOC:	Preparation
POC:	Self-liberation, counterconditioning, helping relationships, social liberation
MI Strategies:	Maintain MI style; assess readiness; remain client-centered; reinforce change talk; empower; support self-efficacy
MI Skills:	Monitor tone of voice, gestures; use OARS; avoid traps; monitor readiness for change; negotiate change plan; ask key questions; offer information and advice
Appropriate for:	Individual session; can be modified for group or family session

Purpose

This activity is designed to create a concrete, measurable, and feasible plan of action with which to guide clients in the process of change.

Introduction

Keep in mind that this activity is frequently used in concert with Activity 1: Goals for Change. Developing a change plan is one of the most important aspects of the preparation stage. As clients consider what they will do to make the changes they desire, generating a change plan encourages them to consider concrete steps they can take toward change. It also gives them a method of evaluating their progress. Your role is to act as guide, helping clients identify achievable steps and assisting them to resolve barriers to change.

In this activity, your focus on the client involves using some Phase 2 strategies (e.g., information and advice, negotiating a plan) and continuing to use OARS, as you will see in both the Activity Steps and the Activity Application sections that follow.

Activity Steps

1. Explain the concept of a change plan and ask permission to proceed with the activity.

2. Ask what important areas the client is willing to write a change plan for (see Activity 1: Goals for Change).

3. Present the change plan format (see Planning for Behavior Change on pages 79–80).

4. As you and the client complete the change plan, continue to use OARS throughout the process.

5. Help the client identify reasons for desired change.

6. Work with the client to generate individual, sequential, and realistic steps.

7. Assist the client to identify barriers to success.

8. Help the client brainstorm solutions to identified barriers.

9. Assist the client in identifying resources available to help her in the process.

10. Assist the client in identifying concrete hallmarks that will let her know she is on track.

Activity Application

1. This activity is a negotiation between counselor and client, so you must be mindful of staying client-centered and not allowing your own biases to interfere or take over. In this way, the client is more likely to accept the plan as her own rather than one that has been imposed on her.

2. Be as clear and specific as possible in order to ensure that the final plan is one that the client understands and can follow after leaving the session.

3. If the client asks for advice at this point in the process of change, you may offer it in a supportive manner. Keeping in mind the style and spirit of MI, be careful that your suggestions avoid giving the impression you know best.

4. Talking about what others in your client's situation have done or discovered, or offering factual information such as a list of Twelve Step meetings, is intended to keep the decision making in the client's court, with you acting as a helpful, well-informed coach.

5. Clients often overestimate the difficulties involved and underestimate the amount of time it will take to complete the steps they identify. Be careful to balance empowering clients to make their own choices with keeping them reality based.

   Also, please note that you can do this activity verbally with clients who do not write.

Planning for Behavior Change

1. Behavior that I would like to modify or change: *(be specific)*

   _____

   _____

2. List the top three reasons for wanting to make the change identified above.

   _____

   _____

   _____

3. Identify the specific steps that will help me accomplish the change I want to make.

   _____

   _____

   _____

   _____

   _____

4. Identify four to five barriers that may get in the way with my ability to accomplish the desired change.

   _____

   _____

   _____

   _____

   _____

continued on other side

5. List the supportive people in my life who will assist in my desired change including how they can be helpful.

Person: _____ can help me by:

_____

_____

Person: _____ can help me by:

_____

_____

Person: _____ can help me by:

_____

_____

6. By making the desired change, I am hoping I will have the following effects:

a. _____

_____

b. _____

_____

c. _____

_____

which will let me know that my plan for change is working.

Activity 3:

Ready, Willing, and Able

SOC:	Preparation
POC:	Self-liberation, counterconditioning, helping relationships, social liberation
MI Strategies:	Maintain MI style; assess readiness; remain client-centered; reinforce change talk; empower; support self-efficacy
MI Skills:	Monitor tone of voice, gestures; use OARS; avoid traps; monitor readiness for change; negotiate change plan; ask key questions; offer information and advice
Appropriate for:	Individual session; can be modified for group or family session

Purpose

This activity will help to determine, with clients who appear stuck, whether their issue is motivation, confidence, or readiness to change. The result gives counselors guidance about which issue to work with first. It also is useful for teaching clients about the complexities of change.

Introduction

Sometimes clients are willing to make changes but are hesitant to do so. They may not know how to proceed, or they may feel incapable of moving forward. At other times, they may have the skills and confidence to change but really don't want to do so. This activity is presented in two parts. Part 1 allows you to identify which issue to begin intervening on with clients who seem to be standing still. Part 2 suggests how to move forward depending on which variable needs to be addressed first.

Clients are usually unaware of the multiple internal facets of change. They can more readily learn about the relationships between motivation, confidence, and readiness by choosing to begin this activity with a nonthreatening topic, one that deals with something they have been thinking about changing but haven't acted on, such as reducing fats in their diet.

An illustration is included with the activity steps on page 83 to help guide you through the process of drawing and interpreting the graphic part of the activity, in which you explore the client's levels of motivation, confidence, and readiness.

Activity Steps

PART 1: IDENTIFYING KEY ISSUES

1. Discuss with the client the concept that, in order to make change, one has to be ready, willing, and able. If one of these three components is missing or not in line with the others, change will be slow in coming.

2. Ask permission to explore this concept as it relates to the client and change.

3. Explain each step as you draw the graph shown on page 83.

4. Draw the two baselines of the graph. Label the vertical line Willing (Motivation) and the horizontal one Able (Confidence).

5. Ask the client to place a dot on the Willing/Motivation line that illustrates how much he wants to make this change (point A on the graph).

6. Ask the client to place a dot on the Able/Confidence line that illustrates how confident he is in his ability to make the change (point B on the graph).

7. From the corner at which the Willing/Motivation and Able/Confidence lines meet on the graph, draw a diagonal line upward that divides the graph in half, as shown. Label this line Readiness.

8. Draw a line from point A on the Willing/Motivation line across the graph from left to right.

9. Draw a line from point B on the Able/Confidence line across the graph from bottom to top.

10. The lowest point at which one of the lines intersects the Readiness line illustrates how truly ready the client is to make the desired change.

11. The graph also illustrates whether Willing/Motivation or Able/Confidence is the issue for the client.

12. Explain that the diagram is an illustration of whether confidence or motivation needs to be addressed first in order for the client to make progress.

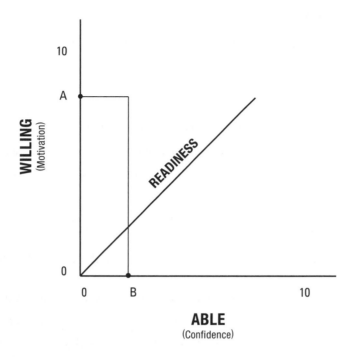

Adapted from *Health Behavior Change: A Guide for Practitioners* by Stephen Rollnick, Pip Mason, and Chris Butler (Churchill Livingstone 1999) 186, with permission from Elsevier.

PART 2: MOVING FORWARD

13. Depending on the results of the graph, make interventions about motivation (willingness) or confidence (ability or skill enhancement) to increase the client's readiness for change. This includes problem solving barriers to change.

In the example above, it is clear that the client has sufficient motivation to change (A), but not enough confidence (B) to do so. In this case, you would spend time developing the client's self-efficacy for change, helping him resolve and increase his sense of capability to make the desired change. Remember that building confidence often involves instilling hope and overcoming self-defeating thoughts or feelings.

Activity Application

1. One way you can help your client build confidence involves teasing out his strengths and successes from past experiences and helping him see how he can apply those skills to the present situation.

2. Remind him that learning is a process. It takes time and practice, and he isn't expected to be able to immediately overcome every obstacle. The next activity, Building Hope for Change, is one way of working with this aspect of confidence.

3. When the issue is one of motivation, your task is to spend time either developing or building and reinforcing your client's desire for change.

4. The importance of creating an atmosphere in the counseling relationship that is accepting and supportive cannot be overstated. Elements of this atmosphere involve your style or approach, carefully listening to your client's reasons for staying the same as well as eliciting both the reasons she may want to consider change and the changes she would consider making, if any.

5. In the context of this "safe" environment, the client will be able to explore and discuss his thoughts and feelings more freely. It is important to communicate to him that he is in charge, and your role is to assist him in his struggle to decide if and/or when he will make a change.

6. Continue to be attentive to the elements and dynamics of change. As you go through this process with your client, take care to stay aware of and alert to her fluctuating level of motivation.

7. Keep in mind the nature and double-sided effects of ambivalence and the ease with which your client can remain "stuck" and feel discouraged.

8. Eliciting change talk throughout this process is important. Remember that strong commitment change talk is predictive of actual change. Keep in mind that your client is more likely to engage in commitment talk after you have identified his values and strengths and have worked to elicit and support his change talk about desires, abilities, reasons, and needs. You might review chapter 2 or appendix A for greater detail.

Activity 4:

Building Hope for Change

SOC:	Preparation
POC:	Self-liberation, counterconditioning, helping relationships, social liberation
MI Strategies:	Maintain MI style; assess readiness; remain client-centered; reinforce change talk; empower; support self-efficacy
MI Skills:	Monitor tone of voice, gestures; use OARS; avoid traps; monitor readiness for change; negotiate change plan; ask key questions; offer information and advice
Appropriate for:	Individual session; can be modified for group or family session

Purpose

This activity operates to increase hope for clients who want to change but may not feel able to do so. It builds on clients' existing strengths and helps them recall skills they have used in earlier circumstances that they may have forgotten or not realized are applicable to their current situation.

Introduction

For many people, the prospect of change is daunting. They may see change as necessary and desirable, but they avoid actually engaging in the change process. For many clients, avoidance is related to their lack of feeling capable of or competent to change.

Sometimes clients actually make sincere attempts to change that are unsuccessful for a variety of reasons. They may have tried the wrong methods, or perhaps they expected the desired change to occur more quickly than is realistic. Something else may have gotten in the way of success. Whatever the reason, the sense of failure that often develops interferes with their process as they convince themselves that they are unable to change even when they try.

Another factor is the reality that changing substance abuse behavior requires a significant lifestyle adjustment. Often clients will say, "I just want to give up the drugs, not alcohol," or "I don't want to change what I do for fun with my using friends." When they realize they can't ignore these issues, and that changing their substance abuse often means making new friends, the task begins to feel like one of too much loss, too soon, and the result can be overwhelming. The conclusion they may reach is "I give up."

Additional information in the Activity Application section will facilitate your implementation of this activity with clients.

Activity Steps

1. Ask the client to recall a change he has successfully made in his life.

2. Ask the client to think about his process of change, including what he had to do to make the change, how he thought about it, what plans he made, and who, if anyone, helped him.

3. Work with the client to generate a list of the strengths he used that resulted in his being successful with the change. See the example on page 87.

4. Then ask the client to recall another time when using these strengths helped with other aspects of his life. Explore with him to reinforce his strengths list.

5. List the client's top three to five strengths.

6. Ask the client to identify the skills he needed to utilize those strengths. Write the skills next to the strengths.

7. Point out that the same skills and strengths he identified can be used or modified to help with the current change. Let him know that this may require building more strengths and skills, and that that is true for most people. This can be accomplished by focusing on the strengths and skills he has already versus what he doesn't possess.

8. Close the session by asking the client to take the list of strengths and skills home and think about them between now and the next session. Invite him to add to the list if he chooses. If he thinks he has the skills needed to develop to make his desired changes, ask him to keep the list for ongoing discussions.

EXAMPLE

Successful Change in the Past: Losing Weight

STRENGTHS	SKILLS
1. Cares about self	• Identifying healthy foods • Planning • Problem solving
2. Persistence	• Able to explore further • Knows pitfalls of giving up • Can track his progress • Can organize and follow structure
3. Patience	• Uses time well • Able to postpone gratification • Able to manage triggers

Activity Application

1. Approach this activity from the perspective of issuing an invitation to clients to explore past successes and identify specific strengths and skills.

2. When you ask a client to choose something he has changed successfully in the past, prompt him to choose something that resulted in him having a sense of accomplishment, such as completing a home/school project, exercising more, or even stopping smoking.

3. Once you move on to generating a list of strengths, your client is very likely to need assistance. Introduce some suggestions by prompting with fill-in-the blank statements such as "I had to know _____," "I was able to _____," "I realized I was _____," until she has generated the list of strengths.

4. Clients also frequently need assistance to identify the skills involved in utilizing their strengths. You can help them think this through by asking detailed questions. For example, if a client indicated that following through on projects was a strength, ask him to examine what he needed to do to follow through on the projects he finished. Questions focused on specifics such as "Did you have to create a plan?" "Did you have to use your thinking skills to overcome barriers within the project?" and "Did you have to use your skills at writing or reading?" will facilitate his ability to identify and label behaviors as skills.

5. This is a fairly straightforward activity that can be completed in many types of counseling sessions. For some people, building hope can be done through the activity itself.

6. For others, completing the activity with the input of others in a group format also offers hope.

7. Reminding people that change is possible, asserting that there is hope for them, and reinforcing that they can do it is of the utmost importance. Remind clients that building hope and confidence requires action, and that when they feel ready to act, this growth will occur. At the same time, point out that they have already shown in previous circumstances that they are able and willing to change.

■

At this point, we have gone through a process of engaging clients in examining and planning for behavior change. You have established a positive counseling relationship, explored clients' pros and cons of change, and collaborated with them to develop an action plan to pursue.

The next chapter offers activities for continuing to assist and monitor your clients' progress as they implement their plans. Other activities help you support their successes and use them to reinforce the changes clients have made.

■ ■ ■

MAINTAINING CHANGE

Everything that has a beginning has an ending.
Make your peace with that and all will be well.

— BUDDHIST SAYING

Maintaining changes and working through relapse are issues of primary importance in the later stages of change. During this phase of the change cycle, clients are benefiting from successes achieved during the action stage of change. However, it is not uncommon for clients to need assistance monitoring the changes they have made, while also managing the success they have experienced.

As with the other stages, a commitment to continued action and alertness to problems that might surface and lead to relapse are essential during the maintenance stage. If a relapse does occur, clients may need help in seeing it as a temporary sidetrack from their path. They need to know they can regain what they have lost. Relapse is not necessarily a failure, but only a step backward. (The chart on page 90 is modified from *Enhancing Motivation for Change in Community Substance Abuse Treatment Programs [TIP 35]*. It lists useful strategies for counselors to pursue with clients who are in the maintenance stage and adds the processes of change relevant at each stage. Since relapse/recycling is a unique aspect of the maintenance stage, motivational strategies to address this are listed separately in the chart.)

Duplicating this page is illegal. Do not copy this material without written permission from the publisher.

89

Appropriate Motivational Strategies for
Maintenance Stage of Change[1]

CLIENT'S STAGE OF CHANGE	MOTIVATIONAL STRATEGIES FOR COUNSELORS
MAINTENANCE STAGE The client has achieved initial goals, such as abstinence, and is now working to maintain gains. **Process of Change** *Reinforcement Management* Celebrating self for changing *Stimulus Control* Managing urges and triggers to use substances *Social Liberation* Identifying and utilizing the supports society offers to change substance use *Helping Relationships* Establishing supportive relationships while changing behavior related to substance use	• Help the client identify and sample drug-free sources of pleasure (i.e., new reinforcers). • Support lifestyle changes. • Affirm the client's resolve and self-efficacy. • Help the client practice and use new coping strategies to avoid a return to use. • Maintain supportive contact (e.g., explain to the client that you are available to talk between sessions). • Develop a "fire escape" plan if the client resumes substance use. • Review long-term goals with the client.
MAINTENANCE—RELAPSE/RECYCLING The client has experienced a recurrence of symptoms and must now cope with consequences and decide what to do next. *(Note: Relapse, if it does occur, will surface during the maintenance stage of change after the individual has had a period of success at changes made.)*	• Help the client reenter the change cycle and commend any willingness to reconsider positive change. • Explore the meaning and reality of the recurrence as a learning opportunity. • Assist the client in finding alternative coping strategies. • Maintain supportive contact.

The three activities in this chapter for clients in the maintenance and recurrence stages of change are

- Triggers and Coping with Them
- Revisiting Plans for Change
- Lifestyle Inventory

The aim of these activities is to help clients deal with triggers, address relapse, and evaluate their need for additional changes while sustaining the ones they have already made. A chart preceding each activity lists stages of change, processes of change, MI skills and strategies, and settings in which the activity is appropriate.

Activity 1:

Triggers and Coping with Them*

SOC:	Action, maintenance
POC:	Counterconditioning, stimulus control, emotional arousal, environmental reevaluation, self-reevaluation, social liberation, reinforcement management
MI Strategies:	Maintain MI style; reinforce self-efficacy; empower; assess readiness for change; affirm efforts at change; encourage movement toward change; offer assistance and guidance; monitor ambivalence
MI Skills:	Monitor tone of voice, gestures; use OARS; avoid traps
Appropriate for:	Individual; can be modified for group or family session

Purpose

In this activity, clients identify the triggers that preceded their substance use and connect them with their perceptions of the positive effects of their substance use. They then develop plans to manage the triggers.

Introduction

Triggers can include emotional, situational, cognitive, sensate, or other cues that "trigger" someone to engage in a particular behavior, such as substance use. Clients are usually not aware of the triggers or stimuli that spur their desire to use substances, nor do they often verbalize the positive effects they think they get from substance use. Once clients have made a decision to change their substance-using behavior, help them identify their triggers and develop methods of resisting the impulse to use. Connecting the perceived positive effects of their use to their triggers sets the stage for developing alternative ways of achieving their desired positive effects. Before beginning this exercise, you will need to explain its purpose and secure your clients' permission to proceed.

---

* This activity is adapted from "New Roads: Assessing and Treating Psychological Dependence," *Journal of Substance Abuse Treatment* by W. R. Miller and T. F. Pechacek (1987, 4:73–77) with permission from Elsevier.

Activity Steps

1. Ask the client for permission to discuss how she manages her triggers or urges to use.

2. Define the term *trigger* with the client and ask if it is consistent with her experience (see the sample definition on page 94).

3. Introduce the Triggers Worksheet. (A sample worksheet illustrating how the first part of the worksheet might be filled in follows these steps. A blank Triggers Worksheet is located at the end of this activity, page 98.)

4. Say, "I'd like you to think about times in the past when you used to be most likely to drink or use drugs."

5. Write each client response or trigger in the triggers column, continuing until all the possible triggers have been explored.

6. Then ask, "When you were using, what did you like about it?"

7. Write each answer in the desired effects column.

8. Encourage the client to fully explore all of the positive effects from past use.

9. Invite the client to review the two lists; then ask, "Do some of the triggers go with some of the effects?"

10. Ask the client to draw a line between triggers and desired effects.

11. Engage the client in a discussion about whether or not the desired effects can be achieved without triggering substance abuse.

12. Discuss with the client the *importance* of having other options to achieve the desired effects, and ask the client if she would like to explore those options.

13. Ask permission to develop a coping plan for one or more of the most common triggers to achieve desired effects.

14. Ask the client to write down the trigger she wants to work with. Write the desired effect on the Triggers Worksheet.

15. Work with the client to brainstorm options for achieving the desired effect and write them down.

16. Ask, "How likely are you to use these options?"

17. Ask, "Who among your family or friends can help you?" Write down the names under Support People on the worksheet.

18. Continue this process until the client understands and recognizes the value of options that would achieve the desired effects while helping her reduce her triggers.

19. Continue this process until the client completes exploring all options.

TRIGGER DEFINITION:

Triggers are emotional or cognitive responses, physical conditions, or
social situations that might lead a person to seek out or use alcohol or drugs.

Note: ————————————————————————————————►

If a client's trigger is going to the bar after work with co-workers, and the desired effect is a feeling of belonging, the possibilities written under Options could be explored.

Testing the reality of the options comes next. In the final step, the client chooses the option most likely to work and identifies the people who will support this new behavior.

Triggers Worksheet — Example

Triggers	Desired Effects
Co-workers going to the bar after work	Relaxation
Smoking a cigarette	Lowered anxiety
Smelling alcohol	Feeling happy
Having a fancy dinner	Feeling of belonging
Getting together with friends	Not caring what anyone thinks
Going fishing	Tranquillity

Trigger (from column above)

Co-workers going to the bar after work

Desired Effects (from column above)

Feeling of belonging

Options for Desired Effects

1. Arranging with another group of friends to meet for coffee after work

2. Going to a support meeting after work

3. Suggesting that co-workers try a new activity, such as going to a movie together

Support People

Sponsor, family doctor, counselor, friend, and family members

Activity Application

1. As clients verbalize their triggers, using reflections will help you avoid assumptions and understand what they are trying to convey.

2. Having a list of coping strategies used successfully by others will provide helpful hints for your clients as they work to think of options for themselves, such as calling support systems, assessing their environment, and avoiding people and situations that involve using. Having such a list of strategies has the added benefit of taking you out of the role of prompting them with possibilities, thereby allowing you to avoid giving the impression that you have all the answers and will simply tell them what to do.

3. Some clients will not see the need to talk about triggers, since they believe they are doing well and don't need any assistance. Nonetheless, it is advisable to engage them in exploring this topic. The conversation itself is an effective method to inquire about your clients' experiences with urges to use and how they have handled them, including what has worked and what has been especially useful.

Group Application

1. This activity can also be done in a group setting with fairly minor alterations. Provide clients with copies of the Triggers Worksheet found on page 98. Begin by leading a group discussion about the term *trigger,* after which you provide a definition such as the one on page 94 for use by the group.

2. Have clients fill out the Triggers and Desired Effects columns individually. Ask clients to volunteer what they wrote in the two columns and write their responses on the board in appropriately labeled columns. Ask if clients see a relationship between any of the triggers and any of the desired effects, and draw lines connecting identified pairs. See the example on page 97.

3. Next, lead a discussion about the importance of the desired effects and the need to have options to achieve them. Choose a desired effect and have the group brainstorm ways of achieving it without the use of drugs. Explore the likelihood of them using the options, and have them write the

realistic ones on their worksheet. Ask the group to brainstorm resources that would support them in behaving in the way they have identified, and have clients write down ideas that would work for them.

4. The activity can end at this point, or clients can work separately or in groups to find alternative approaches to other desired effects they identified. It is also possible to continue working in individual counseling sessions as appropriate.

Group Example

Triggers	Desired Effects
Smelling cigarette smoke	Feeling good
Cravings to drink	Social interaction
Able to sleep	Relaxation

Trigger (from column above)

Smelling cigarette smoke

Desired Effects (from column above)

Relaxation

Options for Desired Effects

1. Deep breathing

2. Massage

3. Yoga

4. Sports

Support People

Triggers Worksheet

Triggers	Desired Effects
1.	
2.	
3.	
4.	

Trigger (from column above)

_____

Desired Effects (from column above)

_____

Options for Desired Effects

1. _____

2. _____

3. _____

Support People

_____

_____

_____

_____

Activity 2:

Revisiting Plans for Change

SOC:	Maintenance
POC:	Counterconditioning, stimulus control, social liberation, environmental reevaluation, self-reevaluation, reinforcement management
MI Strategies:	Maintain MI style; support self-efficacy; help recognize and manage triggers; support problem-solving barriers; assess readiness
MI Skills:	Monitor tone of voice, gestures; use OARS; avoid traps; offer information and advice
Appropriate for:	Individual

Purpose

The subtitle of this activity might be When a Relapse Occurs, since this activity will assist clients who have had episodes of substance use which causes a return to the stage of change they were in when their use occurred.

Introduction

The frequency of relapse or recurrence of substance use is a well-known, though often disheartening, aspect of recovery from addiction. Relapse serves a positive purpose when it can be used to help strengthen clients' understanding and belief that their substance use is detrimental to them and that the relapse does not need to be more than a momentary detour on their desired path.

It is important to normalize any using episode as a learning experience. Remember that a relapse occurrence does not mean a return to the precontemplation stage. For some clients, relapse may be an indication that some part of their change plan is not working effectively. Sometimes the intensity of triggers and urges to use are overwhelming. Perhaps the client and counselor were moving too quickly through the process, or family members were exerting too much pressure for immediate change. The important factor in this activity is that counselor and client revisit the relapse episode to learn from the experience.

Activity Steps

1. Affirm client for coming to the appointment and ask permission to discuss his recent using event.

2. Suggest that one way to look at the episode is to revisit the client's change plan.

3. Ask the client if he would like to explore his change plan.

4. Ask the client to describe what took place during the episode, including when, where, and why it happened and whom he was with at the time.

5. Process the client's response by identifying the issues that caused the client to use. Include any client triggers identified and feelings experienced, especially immediately before and after the use occurred. *Remember to use OARS during this process and to normalize the experience for the client.*

6. Ask how the client handled the feelings, thoughts, and/or triggers. Tease out from him the skills and abilities that helped him cope with the using event. Reflect those back to the client to build hope for continued progress.

7. Complete processing the client's using event by asking him what he learned from this experience, especially what he learned about himself and his coping skills when he was confronted with challenges to maintaining the changes he wanted to make.

8. Remember to reflect, affirm, and elicit throughout as appropriate.

9. Review with the client the options for coping with the triggers noted in his change plan.

10. Work with the client to generate a new list of options for coping with the triggers he identified. Help assure him that they are realistic, and identify areas in which he needs to learn new skills or practice existing skills.

11. Review his support options and address identified issues, such as needing to add new support people or eliminate ones who have been ineffective.

12. Develop an agreement about how you and he will continue to work together for his benefit and identify your next meeting date.

Activity Application

1. Clients who experience episodes of using or a recurrence usually feel guilt and shame about their behavior and lose confidence in their ability to be successful.

2. Help these clients normalize their experience and frame it as an opportunity to experience the impact triggers can have as well as recognize the effect that use has on them.

3. Explain that exploring their behavior, thoughts, and feelings at the time of the incident will help them understand how they rationalize using and thereby get off track from achieving their goals.

4. Check to be sure that the clients' goals continue to include abstinence.

5. The activity is completed when you reinforce the clients' commitment to reengage in the change process, highlighting the strengths clients have to solve their own problems and their ability to overcome barriers to change.

Activity 3:

Lifestyle Inventory

SOC:	Maintenance
POC:	Counterconditioning, stimulus control, social liberation, environmental reevaluation, self-reevaluation, reinforcement management
MI Strategies:	Maintain MI style; support self-efficacy; help recognize and manage triggers; support problem-solving barriers; assess readiness
MI Skills:	Monitor tone of voice, gestures; use OARS; avoid traps; offer information and advice
Appropriate for:	Individual

Purpose

This activity supports clients in the lifestyle changes that they have made or are in the process of making and assists them to evaluate additional needed changes.

Introduction

For clients in the maintenance stage, sustaining the changes they have made is a significant challenge. Many factors arise that endanger the progress made. In this activity, you work with your client to evaluate the changes she has made already. It is important to support, reinforce, and examine those areas she feels are still in need of work.

A helpful tool for this activity is a worksheet that delineates major life areas and includes a rating scale with which a client can rate her improvements (see the sample worksheet, Life Inventory, on page 106).

Activity Steps

1. Introduce the Life Inventory and ask the client to think about any changes that have occurred since she initiated changes in her alcohol/drug use.

2. Ask the client to rate the amount of improvement she has made in each life area.

3. Ask the client to examine the areas in which she has made the most satisfying changes and discuss how she made those changes, what worked, and what specific skills and methods she used. List the skills and methods identified.

4. Ask the client how she plans to continue the changes she has made in these life areas. List her responses.

5. Ask the client to focus on the areas in which she has made the least improvements. There are two options for the next step.

6. *Option A.* If the client is not ready to work on any additional improvements, acknowledge this decision and reinforce the changes made already. Proceed to step 10.

7. *Option B.* If the client chooses an area in which to make additional changes, process the changes with the client (see the option B example on page 104).

8. Process solutions and barriers for change and plan specific steps to take. Use the list of skills and methods generated earlier, in step 3, as an aid to making her desired changes and work with her to generate additional possible methods.

9. Invite the client to choose a few methods to work on. Have her identify the ones that are most attractive and specify what she hopes to accomplish between now and the next meeting.

10. Remind the client of the successes she has already had and reinforce her ability to continue to maintain them.

11. Request permission to call the client midway between now and the next appointment to offer support during this time, if needed.

Duplicating this page is illegal. Do not copy this material without written permission from the publisher.

103

Option B Example

The client identifies creating social support as something she wants to improve.

Explore this change by identifying the client's perception of her motivation, skills, reasons, and need for making this change. The following dialogue is an example of a session in which the desired change is processed.

Client: I think I would like to improve my ability to make social contacts.

Counselor: You are noticing something missing for you in this area of your life.

Client: Yes. Do you have any thoughts about this?

Counselor: Well, let's explore this together.

Client: Okay.

Counselor: Usually when people think about making changes, there are a few areas they need to consider. Shall we take a look at these a little closer?

Client: Great, that would help.

Counselor: Let's take a look at four areas: What motivates your desire for this change, how capable are you to make that change, how important is it to you, and what are the reasons you want change? Where would you like to start?

Client: Well, I could tell you why I want to make this change.

Counselor: Okay. What would you tell me?

Client: I have realized that having contact with others really helps me to feel less depressed. Since my husband has died, I find I need more contact with others, and I like people and being around others.

Counselor: So you already know that your desire for making this change is based on your need to be around others, which seems to make you happier.

Client: Yeah.

Counselor: Well, since you know this already, how confident are you feeling about improving this aspect of your life right now?

Client: Well, I guess this is the area I struggle with the most. I am a little shy and feel uncomfortable with interacting with others.

Counselor: So, something that might help you feel more comfortable is learning to interact with others better. What else would make you feel more comfortable?

Continue to explore the remaining areas, eliciting change talk throughout.

Activity Application

1. The two options provided for in this exercise reinforce the importance of attending to client readiness.

2. Regularly checking your client's readiness to change helps you stay client-centered and keeps you from getting ahead of your client.

3. When your initial focus is on the positive changes your client has made, you are providing her with the support she needs to maintain her new behaviors. Clients at this stage are working to integrate their changes into their lives.

4. Keep in mind that there may be some areas of your client's life that were satisfactory already. Remember to focus on the client's agenda and explore the importance of her choices during this process.

5. Your job during this stage is to reinforce the changes she has already made and to encourage additional changes that will advance her toward her long-term goals.

6. For option B, refer to Activity 2: Developing a Change Plan, in chapter 4, as needed (page 76).

Life Inventory

Rate the amount of improvement that has occurred since you initiated changes in your use of alcohol or other drugs.

Social/Friendships

1	2	3	4	5
No Change	Few Changes	Some Changes	Many Changes	Major Changes

Family

1	2	3	4	5
No Change	Few Changes	Some Changes	Many Changes	Major Changes

Work/School

1	2	3	4	5
No Change	Few Changes	Some Changes	Many Changes	Major Changes

Leisure/Hobbies

1	2	3	4	5
No Change	Few Changes	Some Changes	Many Changes	Major Changes

Health/Mental Health

1	2	3	4	5
No Change	Few Changes	Some Changes	Many Changes	Major Changes

Spiritual

1	2	3	4	5
No Change	Few Changes	Some Changes	Many Changes	Major Changes

Other (Insert desired category)

1	2	3	4	5
No Change	Few Changes	Some Changes	Many Changes	Major Changes

Skills and Methods Used to Make Changes:

Plans for Continuing Change:

We now have helped clients who have made significant life changes solidify those changes. They have achieved many goals, identified and connected with support systems, and planned for relapse prevention. It still is possible for clients in this stage to have a recurrence of use. When that happens, it is important to normalize the event and assist them to evaluate and improve their relapse prevention plan. Minimizing guilt and shame and maximizing hope are of tremendous value in this instance.

Next we look at how MI/SOC can be used in working with three special populations: adolescents, culturally diverse clients, and people with co-occurring disorders.

■ ■ ■

Duplicating this page is illegal. Do not copy this material without written permission from the publisher.

107

SPECIAL POPULATIONS

No one cares what you know, until they know how much you care.

— MICAH

The activities presented thus far have been focused on adult members of the majority population, whose diagnosis is primarily substance abuse or addiction. Many counselors serve clients from various cultures of varying ages with co-occurring disorders. Clearly, we cannot cover all of the issues affecting these populations. What we have chosen to do is address methods of working with three special populations—adolescents, culturally diverse clients, and people with co-occurring disorders. In this chapter, our aim is to acknowledge the importance of recognizing and altering your counseling expectations to address the unique characteristics of the individuals with whom you work, while continuing to operate within the MI/SOC framework.

Before we turn to individual populations, let us take a moment to consider an element common to the treatment of these three groups—engagement. As you have read earlier in this book and surely in other readings in MI and SOC, engagement is crucial in working with all clients. It contributes to their willingness to continue seeing you and to believe your program has something to offer them. In any case, how you interact with clients and encourage their sense of comfort in the initial appointment are key to whether or not they will engage with you in the therapeutic process and in your treatment activities.

Engaging members of special populations involves a thorough understanding of the issues that confront them. Be prepared to take as much time as necessary to communicate that you can and will be sensitive to their uniqueness. These clients frequently come with misinformation about or mistrust of the treatment process. They often have been or felt themselves to be mistreated by authority figures. Some may believe that they will not be respected or cared

Duplicating this page is illegal. Do not copy this material without written permission from the publisher.

109

about by anyone in a position of power or authority. It is important not to minimize or marginalize their concerns. The process you go through to engage them in treatment will have to address these concerns.

The extent to which you communicate an empathic, empowering style consistent with the MI counseling approach is the degree to which the client is likely to feel respected and understood. When you are willing to talk about topics of interest or concern to him other than the primary issue of substance abuse, you are saying, in effect, "I care about you as an individual, not just as a client." This goes a long way toward establishing a trusting environment in which clients can feel freer to explore their substance use and what it means in their lives.

The format of this chapter is a bit different from that of the last three chapters. It is divided into two parts. In the first part, we present a brief discussion of some of the special characteristics of each population, including some thoughts and ideas about effective approaches to counseling these clients. In the second part, we offer several activities for the populations of adolescents and culturally diverse clients. Engaging people with co-occurring disorders presents its own challenge. This population is made up of people who have a broad range of diagnoses, such as ADHD, depression, bipolar disorder, or schizophrenia. It is not possible to choose one or two activities that would apply across the entire range. Instead, we decided to provide a sample case study that illustrates an approach for engaging these clients. To help clarify what the counselor does in the session, we included notes about the counselor's intentions and some of the techniques she uses. We hope this format will illustrate that the approach presented in this book is flexible enough to address the needs of diverse groups of people while retaining its integrity.

Before we discuss treatment activities and assignments, we first will explore the issues and concerns for working with three populations: adolescents, culturally diverse clients, and those with co-occurring disorders.

Approaching Adolescent Clients

Adolescents are in a unique position. They are growing physically and emotionally toward adulthood, but they aren't there yet. They have a difficult time being physically still and are experimenting with social interactions and intimacy. They are subject to the demands of their parents, teachers, and other adults, so they do not have complete control over decisions affecting their lives. They tend to see themselves as powerless, a somewhat realistic assessment. They are responsible *to* others rather than *for* others. They want to be unique and independent, yet they also want to fit in with their peers.

Accordingly, counselors working with adolescents would do well to approach them with a few specific thoughts in mind. Probably the most important element to consider is how you feel about adolescents. If you don't like or are uncomfortable with youth in this stage of development, don't work with them. Their radar will quickly pick up your attitude. They will shut down or shut you out, frustrating all concerned and leaving you unable to be effective. If you like and want to work with adolescent clients, keep your sense of humor in the forefront. It will help you relate to them and maintain your perspective in the bargain.

Begin the task of establishing rapport with these thoughts in mind: One aspect of considerable importance is letting them know what information you are required to give others, such as parents or probation officers, and what information you can keep between the two of you. Tactfully but directly addressing "unmentionable" subjects such as sex or substance use lets them know that they can talk freely and openly. Also, it is useful for you to know what kind of music young people are listening to, who their favorite personalities are, some current slang, and other elements of what is important to young people in your area.

Parents, family members, and other important caregivers should be involved whenever possible. The adolescents you work with are and will continue to be part of their households and affected by the attitudes, beliefs, and actions of these adults. As important as peers are at this stage of development, adolescents do care deeply about their families and respond to the influences of their home environments. Also, to develop a more thorough understanding of your client, learn how parents and other family members view the situation. Keep in mind, however, that adolescents are often more free to speak their minds and reveal information when parents or caregivers are not present. Be sure to set aside session time that allows you to see youth without their parents present. This lets them know you are interested in them as individuals and in working toward what they want to accomplish as distinct from their parents' or other significant adults' desires for them.

Duplicating this page is illegal. Do not copy this material without written permission from the publisher.

111

Most adolescents need to be physically active. Organize your time with them to allow for concrete projects or developmentally appropriate activities in addition to conversation alone. Be sure to evaluate the cognitive capacity of your clients before expecting them to respond to theoretical constructs or conceptual activities. Adolescents typically do not think that treatment is necessary for them. Usually, an adult such as a probation officer, school official, or parent has insisted that they participate in treatment. They engage best when they can see the relationship between getting what they want and satisfying the requirements of the referring adult. So getting to that point is crucial for treatment to be effective.

For teens, talking directly about their use is often uncomfortable and, in their eyes, unnecessary. Thus, the possibility of successfully completing an activity, such as establishing treatment goals, is based on the assumption that the counselor has done a sufficient job of engaging them in the program, ensuring that they have become ready to explore how participating in treatment is to their advantage.

Many of the activities in chapters 3–5 can be modified to be appropriate to the developmental processes of teens. We have included four activities for use with adolescents and their families: Establishing Rapport with Teens, Identifying Strengths, Picking Treatment Goals, and Consequences of Using. The first three are designed to engage adolescents in treatment. Until engagement is accomplished, effective treatment cannot occur. These activities build on each other, beginning with an adolescent-specific version of establishing rapport. The next step is to build the adolescents' self-efficacy through identifying their strengths as they work with the developmental task of developing a sense of self. Once this activity has been successfully completed, clients are ready for the third one, Picking Treatment Goals, which starts them participating in the treatment process.

The final activity, Consequences of Using, is a family activity that is done in a group setting with other families. This activity was proposed by John Hahn, with whom we worked to refine it. Families report that participating in the activity helped them recognize the pressures and issues that their teen faces with others, as well as develop an appreciation for how their struggles within their families are often similar to the struggles of other families. The term *parents* is intended here to include caretakers such as foster parents, grandparents, other relatives, and other significant adults.

The next population we consider is clients of culturally diverse backgrounds.

Approaching Culturally Diverse Clients

Many people have studied and written about the sociological and psychological effects of culture and ethnicity on human behavior. We encourage you to explore the wealth of information available about this topic. For your consideration, we offer here some thoughts about issues involving culturally diverse clients and some hints for working with them.

You will need to be as knowledgeable as possible about the history and culture of the population you are seeing. It is important to know the common experiences that culturally diverse people have with the dominant culture in order to understand how to approach and engage prospective clients. Knowing and appreciating their cultural values and beliefs helps position you as a person who understands them and can be trusted.

An overriding issue for culturally diverse people in our society is power and the lack of it. Clients often feel as though they are at a disadvantage and do not have the ability to act in ways that have an impact on their lives or their circumstances. They may think that they and members of their cultural group are looked down on or seen as "less than" by the dominant culture. This can result in their feeling vulnerable and ineffective. When working with these clients, give frequent and consistent messages that they are ultimately in charge. Communicating that you wish to partner with them in their process of attaining their goals is essential to engaging them in treatment. This is especially true if your program does not resemble their cultural group in staff makeup or in its use of other elements, such as pictures, music, or other materials. Incorporating elements that reflect their ethnic background, however, can help clients feel at home in your program's setting.

When you offer information and advice, make a special effort to ensure that your clients want it and that you are not playing the "expert" role. Keep in mind that in some cultures, the locus of control is thought to come from outside the individual—in particular, within the community—meaning that individuals are considered to have little control over or choices about behavior. This includes cultures in which members believe that men "know" and women "serve." Empowering people from this kind of belief system, particularly women, is likely to be a slow and challenging process.

Duplicating this page is illegal. Do not copy this material without written permission from the publisher.

113

Respect for clients' cultures includes understanding their communication patterns. Even within cultures, the nuances of communication are not always clear. People have different styles and paces. People of diverse cultural backgrounds often tell stories to get a point across and use symbolic language. Their hand gestures, pacing, or emotional expressions may be different from your style and approach. It is important to understand the meaning of the communication forms and patterns of your clients so that you can accurately interpret what they are attempting to express. Also, your ability to sensitively and appropriately use culturally specific speech patterns or expressions will convey a message of respect and caring.

Building relationships with culturally diverse clients, particularly people of color, is necessary to make working with them possible and more effective. Their sense of your being connected with them must be nurtured and reinforced by behaviors that express your knowledge of and concern for them in their cultural context. Be sure to acknowledge the reality of conflicts between their culture and the dominant culture. Knowing that you are aware of these conflicts helps clients address them with you. Relating past experiences and stories about others with whom your clients can identify can help them make changes or handle conflicts.

We have found that MI/SOC approaches seem to be a natural fit with culturally specific programs. Many of these programs have accepted and embraced this approach. It is empowering, highly respectful, and empathic, and it encourages counselors to be sensitive to clients' values, beliefs, and internal motivations as well as other aspects of their worldview.

We have chosen two activities, Working through Cultural Discrepancies and Developing a Positive Cultural Identity, that have been used effectively to enhance the self-efficacy of culturally diverse, substance-abusing clients and to help them begin to resolve discrepancies they have with the dominant culture. The activities may be used together or separately and in either individual or group settings. They can be effective with adolescents as well as adults, since they address developmental issues such as creating a sense of self that includes the client's cultural view instead of only the view of the dominant adult world. Furthermore, the activities can be adapted for use with a variety of client populations whose views differ from the dominant culture's.

The activities for culturally diverse clients were originally developed by Miguel Tellez, with whom we worked to refine them. They have been used extensively in his program with Latino youth. His clients often report that participating in the activities helped open their eyes to cultural elements and influences they had not considered. The activities were also beneficial to them in other ways. Care providers for clients from ethnically diverse cultures have reported that the activities are very popular with their clients and have facilitated building rapport and understanding between them and their clients.

Finally, let's explore some of the characteristics, issues, and challenges involved in treating clients who have co-occurring disorders.

Approaching Clients with Co-Occurring Disorders

Like other clients who belong to special populations, those suffering from the co-occurring issues of substance abuse and mental illness respond well to the MI counseling style and approach. These clients can make up as much as 30 to 60 percent of the total population served in any given mental health or substance abuse treatment agency. Research has found that clients with co-occurring disorders (COD) often do not respond well to traditional treatment models and may not enter treatment until their issues become very severe or life threatening.[1] Many of the symptoms they exhibit include chronic joblessness, homelessness, dealing with detox issues, isolation, disaffiliation, and trust problems.

COD clients who do enter treatment often drop out early, experience a return of their symptoms of mental illness, or continue to use substances to manage their COD issues with devastating consequences. A primary reason for the dropout rate is that program services are not designed to address these clients' multiple needs. When clients enter substance abuse treatment, abstinence is not their first priority. Most often, they want relief from their mental health and substance abuse symptoms, which may mean reducing their substance use to a more manageable level. In their experience, using substances such as alcohol or marijuana aids them in symptom reduction. If the main program philosophy or belief is an abstinence-based one—in which the only measure of success is no drinking and attention is given to action-oriented activities such as getting a sponsor, attending self-help groups, and actively pursuing recovery—the client may feel incapable of achieving these goals and drop out of treatment early, feeling even more rejected and depressed. When their symptoms increase in severity, clients suffering with co-occurring disorders can return to the treatment agency in worse shape due to the evolution of their abuse and/or dependency or the lack of adequate treatment for their depression, anxiety, or other issues.

Traditional treatment agencies often have neither equipped their staff nor designed their treatment regimen to address clients who present with mild to severe symptoms of mental illness. Both the Report to Congress on the Prevention and Treatment of Co-occurring Substance Abuse Disorders and Mental Disorders and Best Practices Concurrent Mental Health and Substance Use Disorders recommend that organizations serving clients with COD issues become dual diagnosis capable.[2] This includes ensuring that clients receive the care they need in a compassionate, caring manner that normalizes their experiences in life as they struggle to overcome multiple problems.

Osher and Kofoed propose a stages model of treatment for persons with co-occurring disorders that fits well with MI/SOC.[3] Clients in the first stage, engagement, do not recognize that a problem exists, much like clients in the precontemplation stage of change. Interventions by family members or others related to their use or abuse can encourage clients to begin looking at their substance use, thereby encouraging them to engage in the treatment process. The goal for this stage is to create a relationship with identified clients so that they begin to see that getting help for their problems will be productive for them. Caregivers will need to help with areas such as housing assistance, crisis intervention, involvement of families, and working in the clients' own environment. The second stage of the model, persuasion, includes engaging clients in a treatment process that empowers them and normalizes, accepts, and nurtures their view of reality. Part of this stage involves gradually raising clients' doubts about their use and identifying how their goals and values in life may be compromised by their use of alcohol or other drugs. It includes addressing their medication needs, assessing their mental health status, and working toward stabilizing them, educating family members, and providing structure, perhaps in an intensive outpatient day treatment setting. The style and spirit of MI is a natural fit with this stage.

The other two stages, active treatment and relapse prevention, are devoted to ongoing recovery. At this time, it is necessary to support clients' efforts at abstinence and handle relapse issues while encouraging gains in recovery. Osher and Kofoed point out the important role of stabilization for these clients. Counselors must address the potential for suicidal or homicidal behavior, explore needs for medication, and address any detox issues. At the same time, they must ensure that clients are able to communicate, especially with care-givers. Ideally, clients should be able to function in an outpatient setting as well as in a hospital setting. Modifications of MI/SOC will need to be made as with other special population groups, but enhancing the care of clients with COD will improve their chances of long-term recovery and health.

What does it mean for counselors to "persuade" clients with co-occurring disorders? In chapter 8 of *Addictions Treatment: A Strengths Perspective* by Katherine van Wormer and Diane Rae Davis, Motivational Interviewing is cited as the most promising approach when working with COD clients who are in the persuasion phase of treatment. Working with clients to ease them into the process of recovery sometimes means that providers are willing to be realistic with clients who present with COD issues. Ensuring abstinence, the authors state, is a good long-term goal. "Because persons with coexisting disorders often present with disorganization, confusion, and a past history of unhelpful professional contacts and may live in an environment oppressed by poverty, violence, and ongoing substance misuse, it is understandably difficult for them to engage and remain active in a treatment process."[4]

It is beyond the scope of this book to address the many types of dual disorders that exist and the multiple facets of engaging these clients. We encourage the reader to pursue both research literature and books such as the one identified above to find specific information on the types of dually disordered clients with whom they are working. In addition, in the case study at the end of this chapter, we offer some suggestions and ideas about engaging clients suffering from a combination of mental health and substance abuse issues using the MI counseling style and strategies. The following material includes activities for adolescents, families, and culturally diverse clients, as well as a case study of a client with a co-occurring disorder.

Duplicating this page is illegal. Do not copy this material without written permission from the publisher.

117

Activities for Adolescents and Families

Three adolescent activities and one family activity are included on the following pages. The activities are

- Establishing Rapport with Teens
- Identifying Strengths
- Picking Treatment Goals and
- Consequences of Using

Adolescent Activity 1:

Establishing Rapport with Teens

SOC:	Precontemplation
POC:	Consciousness raising
MI Strategies:	Maintain MI style, build rapport and trust, engage client, remain client-centered, monitor resistance, be sensitive to developmental issues, use teen-friendly language
MI Skills:	Monitor tone of voice, gestures; use OARS; elicit client concerns; avoid traps
Appropriate for:	Individual session; can be modified for group or family session

Purpose

This activity is designed to create an environment in which adolescents feel comfortable with the counseling setting.

Introduction

One of the earliest and most important aspects of counseling is establishing a relationship with clients. From the very first contact, counselors work to create a collaborative, trusting environment in which clients are encouraged to become active partners with their counselors in the treatment process. Goals that may be realistic for an initial interview with adults (establishing rapport, asking permission to explore change, and building a trusting relationship in which potential treatment goals can be addressed in collaboration) are likely to be too ambitious when working with adolescents. Establishing rapport may take two to three meetings. Talking about change or working on an agenda that addresses change may not happen for several weeks. Slowing down the process and taking the time to address the adolescent client's needs are essential for successful treatment.

The concept of partnering with a teen can be challenging. Teens often feel a lack of power to exercise their choices, especially with an adult. This activity illustrates how a counselor might approach working with a teen to increase collaboration and trust. Since the first contact with clients is frequently an assessment, the activity is presented here as an assessment session. While this activity is designed for the client in precontemplation, it can be used with clients at any stage of change.

This first activity is presented in three parts: opening the session, counselor/ agency agenda (for example, gathering data), and closing the session.

Activity Steps

PART 1: OPENING THE SESSION

1. Greet the client.

   a. Use his first name and establish eye contact if culturally appropriate.

   b. Offer choices of seating to let the teen know you are interested in his choices.

   c. Ask a question designed to put him at ease, such as "How is your day going so far?" or "Are you feeling a little nervous about this appointment?"

2. Start the session with an open-ended question, such as "What brings you here today?" or "What were you told about this meeting today?"

3. Reflect responses.

4. Clarify the reasons for the visit.

5. Ask the client if he has concerns about what will happen to the information he gives you today (see the note on page 121 about confidentiality).

6. Next, request permission to move on to completing the assessment.

7. Invite the teen to ask questions about what will happen. *Remember to use OARS, especially reflective listening.*

8. Ask if there is something specific he would like to get from the appointment.

PART 2: COUNSELOR/AGENCY AGENDA

1. Remind the client that you now will have to gather some information, so you will need to ask questions during this part of the process.

2. Ask permission to continue.

3. Proceed using your organization's assessment forms.

PART 3: CLOSING THE SESSION

1. Summarize the key points the client made in the session.

2. Based on this, offer your initial impressions about his situation. Take care to avoid labeling.

3. Provide options for the next steps and ask the client how he wants to proceed.

4. Be sure to offer him options for proceeding with family and/or caregivers.

Activity Application

1. Initial greeting of clients sets the environment for the interview, letting them know you are interested in them and their experience, and that they will have some choices in this situation.

2. A discussion about confidentiality, when handled with sensitivity, is an excellent way to demonstrate respect to the adolescent and convey your intention to be collaborative and "kid" friendly.

   Note: Confidentiality is a bigger issue for adolescents than it is for adults. Young people often fear that anything they say can and will be used against them by the adults in their lives, especially parents or others who have control over their lives, such as school officials or probation officers. It is essential to spend a significant amount of time clarifying the boundaries around confidentiality as well as explaining to clients what they should expect from you, what their rights are, and how they will be respected.

3. Asking adolescents what they want from the interview continues the engagement process and lets them know that they are not powerless and left to their family's or referring agent's agenda alone.

4. Offering choices or options about the level of intensity of treatment the clients want enhances the sense that this is a collaborative process.

5. Adolescents are particularly inquisitive about what will happen if they take a urine test that they know will be positive. A response that furthers

engagement involves letting them know you are obliged to inform their family members, but you would prefer that *they* make that report within a certain time frame, such as a week. As you negotiate this option, you should ask them how they might be able to submit a clean sample. This strategy continues to engage and empower the teens, while letting them know that there are consequences to their choices.

6. Adolescents are more likely than adults to deny permission to continue. When this happens, your role is to accept their decision while helping them understand the consequences by asking questions such as "What would you like me to tell your parents about your decision?" or "If your parole officer calls, is there something specific you want me to say from your point of view?"

7. In this way, you continue to negotiate what you will and will not do and allow the clients to make choices about what they want to pursue.

8. Conclude the session by asking how the clients felt and if they would feel comfortable coming back in the future, if their circumstances change.

9. Even in ordinary circumstances, adolescents are frequently resistant to adult authority figures. Your skills at managing resistance will be called on regularly. Paying attention to avoiding the traps discussed in chapter 2, such as labeling, premature focus, or taking sides, helps keep you focused on the needs and wants of adolescents.

10. Young people are very sensitive to the words and actions of adults and can quickly disengage over a casual remark that labels them, such as using the words *drug abuser, dropout,* or *juvenile offender.*

Adolescent Activity 2:

Identifying Strengths

SOC:	Precontemplation
POC:	Consciousness raising
MI Strategies:	Maintain MI style; build rapport and trust; engage client, remain client-centered; monitor resistance; be sensitive to developmental issues; use teen-friendly language
MI Skills:	Monitor tone of voice, gestures; use OARS; elicit client concerns; avoid traps
Appropriate for:	Group or family session; can be modified for individual session

Purpose

This activity provides an opportunity for adolescents to discover and acknowledge some of their strengths, thereby building self-efficacy and enhancing their sense of self while also attending to developmental issues related to individuation.

Introduction

Adolescents are in the process of growing and learning about themselves. Through their life experiences, they are making decisions about who they are, what they are capable of, and where they fit in the world. Frequently, those decisions are based on an incomplete understanding of themselves and their capacities. Learning to recognize, acknowledge, and identify their strong points is important for them as they develop a sense of self-efficacy and gain confidence in their ability to affect their own lives and have an impact on the world they live in.

Developing an identity, a sense of self, is a developmental task of adolescence. The aim of this activity is for clients to recognize that developing a realistic sense of who they are and what worldview they adopt requires self-evaluation. Part of that self-evaluation involves evaluating their strengths. To do this, clients will need feedback from others. Ideally, this feedback will enable them to identify their own unique characteristics, such as honesty or the ability to get along well with others. This increases their self-esteem (self-efficacy).

Duplicating this page is illegal. Do not copy this material without written permission from the publisher.

123

In working through the task of developing an identity, many teens think that a drug-using lifestyle defines who they are as a person. In fact, using drugs is something they do for a variety of reasons, but is not who they are. Once they begin to develop a broader identity, they will be able to define themselves from the perspective of more than one life area.

This activity is presented for an adolescent group format, which allows clients to interact with others their own age and learn from the responses of other group members. While best done in conjunction with other youth and family members, it also can be done in individual sessions. If you have clients who do not read, you can read the questions out loud and ask group members or individual clients to respond.

Activity Steps

1. Distribute the Finding My Talents and Skills worksheet (see page 126).

2. Ask the group to choose two to three questions they would be willing to answer out loud.

3. Model the behavior desired by giving an example, such as by asking the group question 11.

4. Invite the group to respond to that question.

5. Once the group responds, ask a client to choose one question from the list identified earlier to ask the group.

6. Coach the client throughout this process.

7. The group responds.

8. When the group has finished responding, the client picks another group member, who then chooses a question to read and have the group answer.

9. Continue until all group members have had at least one turn, or continue until the time is up.

10. Present an informal talk about the part that knowing your strengths plays in feeling good about yourself.

Activity Application

1. Adolescents are in the process of developing social skills. This activity can help them practice appropriate ways of relating to each other and learn from the examples of other group members. They can enjoy each other's company at the same time that they divulge information that can be used to build their sense of self.

2. They also receive feedback about how others see their strengths. Group members usually share a lot of information during this activity.

3. Establish a group environment in which it is easy for teens to share themselves with others. Make sure the atmosphere encourages young people to feel accepted and listened to by you and the others in the group.

4. Focus on observing the process and keeping the teens on task without interfering with positive social outlets.

5. The key is to steer the conversation toward recognizing the strengths their experiences reveal. Reinforce any change talk made, repeat comments from the group that build on the abilities of the group members, and reinforce behaviors and verbalizations that help them build a positive sense of self.

6. The counselor should let the group members know that an important part of feeling good about themselves is developing a positive sense of self. Learning about and recognizing their strengths are key elements of the sense of self, which will influence the kinds of decisions teens make about their behavior.

7. Discuss with the group how self-confidence and necessary skills are related to being willing and able to change.

Finding My Talents and Skills

Below are some questions that can help adolescents identify some of their abilities and strengths. Pick a few questions you would be willing to talk about with others during the group session.

1. How do you show others you care about them?

2. Whom have you stood up to about your beliefs, and how did you do it?

3. How do you share your talents and skills with others?

4. What are some ways that being successful in school will help you in your future?

5. What are your talents and special skills?

6. How has telling the truth made a difference in your life?

7. Think of a time when a friend wanted you to do something you thought was wrong, and you did not do it. Describe what happened and how you felt afterward.

8. Identify your most important goal in life. What is it and how do you plan to meet it?

9. When did you help a friend solve a problem that was important and difficult for him or her? How did you feel and how did your friend respond?

10. How do you handle conflicts in your life?

11. What do you feel hopeful about in your life?

12. What do your friends and family tell you about your talents, skills, and strengths?

13. As you think about the values you have, how do you find yourself living up to those values?

14. Tell us a story about your family that tells us something about you.

15. What worries or concerns do you have in your life today?

Adolescent Activity 3:

Picking Treatment Goals

SOC:	Precontemplation
POC:	Consciousness raising
MI Strategies:	Maintain MI style; build rapport and trust; engage client; remain client-centered; monitor resistance; be sensitive to developmental issues; use teen-friendly language
MI Skills:	Monitor tone of voice, gestures; use OARS; elicit client concerns; avoid traps
Appropriate for:	Group or family session; can be modified for individual session

Purpose

This activity gives adolescents a chance to talk about their own goals for change. It also facilitates their engagement in treatment.

Introduction

The activity is presented here in a group format, although it is possible to use it in individual settings. The previous activities, in which rapport was established and strengths were identified, prepare the way for adolescents to become involved in choosing what they want out of treatment. There are many possibilities. Treatment can satisfy referring adults and fulfill the youths' need to make their own decisions. It can help them make new friends who can support them in evaluating the effect current friends have on their troubles. Learning factual information can help them consider whether their current level of use is still attractive given the consequences they are experiencing. Educating teens in the early phase of treatment, while tying their needs to the ways in which treatment can assist them, is crucial as they enter the treatment process.

Activity Steps

1. Tell the clients that they will be looking at what they want from treatment and how their goals can be met.

2. Hand out the Establishing My Goals worksheet (see pages 130–32) and ask clients to fill out the items on the worksheet individually. Assist those

who may have difficulty completing the worksheet due to poor reading or writing skills.

3. When clients have completed the worksheet, ask them to report their findings to the larger group.

4. As group members report their responses, write them on a board visible to all, placing them under columns labeled Short Term and Long Term.

5. Ask the clients to reflect on these lists.

6. Then, ask the clients whether any of the goals can be accomplished during treatment.

7. Ask the clients if they are ready to choose some goals to develop into their treatment plans.

8. Ask the clients to write these goals down for use in a treatment-planning session.

9. Schedule treatment-planning sessions with clients.

Activity Application

1. Anticipate providing a lot of facilitation during the written portion of the activity, as adolescents often are confused about what they should put down on paper.

2. The worksheet serves as a useful guide for discussion and helps enable group members to develop one or more goals for themselves.

3. If a client is not ready to finalize a plan, completion of this activity can be challenging. As you work with adolescents to plan their treatment, be sensitive to their readiness for change. Although the process may seem slow, if you stay sensitive to your clients' readiness to change, they usually will be able to come up with something they are willing to work on during treatment.

4. It can be beneficial to do this activity in a group with adolescents in different stages of change. For example, working with an older teen who is developing a plan for stopping use may influence a younger teen to consider altering her pattern of use.

5. Regardless of group makeup, approach this group in a collaborative manner, creating an open environment for discussion and summarizing the activity at the end. Be sure that you continue to reinforce change talk and use MI skills and strategies to affirm completion of the task, reflect group members' responses, and support their self-efficacy for change.

Establishing My Goals

1. Describe what brought you to treatment.

   _____

   _____

   _____

   _____

2. Below are categories that can help you think about what you would like to get out of treatment. Please list the one goal you would like to reach in the next three to five months. Skip the lines that do not apply to you.

   Family: _____

   School: _____

   Legal: _____

   Health: _____

   Work: _____

   Leisure: _____

   Substance issues: _____

   Mental health: _____

   Peers: _____

   Other: _____

3. From the list above, identify the two goals that are most important to you today.

   1. _____

   2. _____

   continued on next page

4. Would you be willing to address these two goals as part of your treatment plan? Please answer YES or NO and explain your answer below.

_____

_____

_____

_____

5. Look at the list under question 2 again. Repeat the exercise, but this time allow yourself a year to complete your goal(s). How would your goals change?

Family: _____

School: _____

Legal: _____

Health: _____

Work: _____

Leisure: _____

Substance issues: _____

Mental health: _____

Peers: _____

Other: _____

List the top two goals for yourself that may take up to one year.

1. _____

2. _____

continued on next page

6. Of these longer-term goals, would you be able to use your treatment experience to help you achieve one or both of these goals? Please answer YES or NO and explain your answer below.

_____

_____

_____

_____

_____

_____

_____

_____

_____

Family Activity 4:

Consequences of Using

SOC:	Precontemplation
POC:	Consciousness raising
MI Strategies:	Maintain MI style; build rapport and trust; engage client; remain client-centered; monitor resistance; be sensitive to developmental issues; use teen-friendly language
MI Skills:	Monitor tone of voice, gestures; use OARS; elicit client concerns; avoid traps
Appropriate for:	Group or family session; can be modified for individual session

Purpose

This activity provides a safe way in which youth can inform their families about their experiences with drug use and confront the impact of their use on their family members. Recognizing the consequences of their drug use creates an opportunity to help youth decide to change their behavior.

Introduction

Developmentally, adolescents are trying to separate from their families while they continue to be deeply influenced by them. Sometimes, they are not honest with their family members about the extent of their drug use, a circumstance that has driven a wedge between them and their families. They often are oblivious to or tell themselves they don't care about what others think, especially parents or other family members. The likelihood of successful outcomes increases when counselors help families create an environment that encourages open and honest communication among members and provides opportunities and skills for supporting desirable changes.

This activity is presented in a multiple family group format with the identified client in each family being an adolescent. The format requires youth to talk about their substance use with people other than their own family members. Family members benefit from the fact that youth are likely to be more open with people other than their family members about their substance use. In addition, teens discover the impact substance use has on their family. Eventually, the information is transmitted to the group as a whole so that each family indirectly gets information about its youth and each youth indirectly gets information about how her use affects her family. This activity requires that you use the Consequences of Using worksheet (see page 137). For the sake of brevity, the term *parent* here includes other caregivers.

Activity Steps

1. Explain that the group will explore the consequences of clients' use on themselves and their families.

2. Hand out the Consequences of Using worksheet, explain its use, and go through it with participants, informing them that the results will be shared with the group as a whole at the end of the interviews.

3. Ask the clients to choose a family other than their own to "adopt" for this activity.

4. Ask the clients and adoptive families to group together so they can talk and see each other easily. Urge participants to record responses during the interviews in order to report back later.

5. First, parents will interview the adolescent using part 1 of the worksheet.

6. Next, adolescents will interview the parents using part 2 of the worksheet.

7. While the subgroups are conducting their interviews, prep for the report by putting the headings from the worksheet on a board so that all can see the responses.

8. Observe the subgroups to see when the last one is finished.

9. Ask the clients' permission to report their responses. See the Activity Application section for what to do if a youth denies permission.

10. First, ask the adoptive parents, one by one, to report the youths' responses. Record them in a visible location.

11. Then, ask the biological parents to respond to the adopted family's information about their child. Ask them to share their thoughts, feelings, or ideas.

12. After part 1 responses have been reported and responded to, repeat the process focusing on the parents' responses to the adolescents' interviews in part 2.

13. Process the activity with the group, ending with questions such as "Did the youths know how much impact they were having on their parents or family?" "Does the group believe the youths were honest in their individual consequence reports?" "Do you think people were sincere?" "How do you feel about the information shared?"

14. Summarize the key points in the activity, encouraging continuation of change talk from the whole group.

Activity Application

1. To set the stage for this activity, have materials on clipboards with pencils before the group begins. After the adolescents have "adopted" a family, begin with an open-ended question to help the group warm up.

   Possibilities include "What is one thing you like to do?" or "What is one thing you appreciate about your parent (or other significant person present)?"

2. Ensure that each family subgroup is seated facing each other and will not be disturbed by other groups, and that parents have the Consequences of Using worksheet. In part 2, when adolescents are taking notes, be prepared to help them get their thoughts down on paper, as this is often difficult for youth at this age.

3. This activity effectively engages family members and their teens in discussions of drug use that ordinarily would be difficult for them to participate in together. When young people offer sensitive information about the consequences they experienced, be sure to get their permission before asking them for clarification or to explore further. You are modeling for parents how to approach their teens when talking about topics that deal with sensitive information. Parents need to respect adolescents saying "no" to requests for further exploration or information. Be prepared to assist as needed. For example, if the youth denies permission, explore her reasons

and accept her decision. Then check in with her family members to offer support and any clarification needed.

4. Toward the end of the group session, summarize the activity, noting that, often, participants share more than they expected. Let them know this is a common experience. Reassure group members that their behavior was normal, appropriate, and useful by offering praise and affirmation for taking the risks they took.

5. Finally, be sure to warn parents not to interrogate their adolescents about anything they might have revealed during the session. Point out the implications such cross-examination can have for losing trust and damaging future opportunities for open and honest communication.

Consequences of Using

Part 1

Parents interview teens about their drug and alcohol use. Determine how their use affected their lives by having the teens complete the following statements:

a. The worst consequence from using was _____.

b. The scariest time I had while I was using was _____.

c. The most surprising thing that happened while I was using was

_____.

d. The problem that has lasted the longest due to my using has been

_____.

e. What I feel the most guilty about is _____.

Part 2

The teen will interview the parents. Ask the parents how their own son's or daughter's substance use affected them. Ask the following questions:

a. How did you, as a parent, feel or what did you think about your child's usage?

b. Did you, as a parent, have any health problems resulting from the usage?

c. Did you lose time from work? What problems might this have caused?

d. If you have other children, how did this affect them within your family?

Duplicating this page for personal or group use is permissible.

137

Activities for Culturally Diverse Clients

The two activities in this section are

- Working through Cultural Discrepancies
- Developing a Positive Cultural Identity

Activity 1:

Working through Cultural Discrepancies

SOC:	Precontemplation
POC:	Consciousness raising
MI Strategies:	Maintain MI style; build rapport and trust; engage client; remain client-centered; monitor resistance; be sensitive to cultural issues; use language appropriate to client experiences and comprehension
MI Skills:	Monitor tone of voice, gestures; use OARS; elicit client concerns; avoid traps
Appropriate for:	Individual session; can be modified for group or family session

Purpose

The purpose of this activity is to create an environment in which culturally diverse clients can explore and resolve culture-related struggles and their relationship to substance abuse.

Introduction

Many people from minority groups do not have an appreciation for their cultural history, values, and beliefs, or for the full spectrum of their cultural background. They may grow up in the dominant culture without having their own cultural frame of reference in their schools, their communities, or sometimes even in their own families. The fact that their language and customs differ from those of the dominant culture may affect their family, social, or community life. In addition, they may suffer from isolation due to family or peer substance abuse or mental health issues. Some may even believe that their use of substances is acceptable behavior.

Feelings of shame about having problems frequently prevent families from accessing the services they need. When they do seek outside help, they may experience barriers in society or norms within their primary culture that limit their self-disclosure. Consequently, they may align themselves with a drug- or alcohol-related lifestyle to cope with life pressures or as a way to establish themselves culturally.

When they do not understand or appreciate their cultural background, people of diverse cultural backgrounds, especially youth, may turn to a drug-using subculture to establish a sense of identity. In addition, many clients have had negative experiences with the dominant culture. Their use may be a response to discrimination or isolation, or it may be an angry reaction to injustices they have encountered. They may feel confusion, anger, or sadness about their own cultural background. If they then conclude something is wrong with them or their heritage, they may feel limited about their possibilities in life and begin to make poor choices about their behavior or their future. Often, they may behave in ways that increase their sense of isolation and lower their self-esteem.

An understanding of the concepts of cultural assimilation and acculturation is essential to this activity. For our purposes, *cultural assimilation* is defined as the abandonment of one's first culture in favor of the second culture, which then dominates. *Acculturation* is defined as the process of learning a second culture, in which the second culture is gradually acquired. That is followed by a state of equilibrium in which both cultures play a role in the acculturated person's life.

Counselors must have a good understanding of their clients' cultural background. It is important to convey an exploratory, sympathetic attitude throughout the exercise, especially if you are or appear to be a member of the dominant culture. Remember to stay grounded in the Motivational Interviewing counseling style and be aware of clients' readiness for change.

Introduce the activity by saying that people who come to the United States from other countries have in common the experience of cultural discrepancies. Say that you would like to explore some of the discrepancies that the clients in this group often encounter and what that can mean to them. Ask permission to proceed. Please note that a diagram is included at the end of this activity to aid in your understanding of the activity steps and the use of visual aids (see pages 143–44).

Many of the terms and examples used are based on Latino culture. With changes to reflect the cultural population you are working with, this activity can be used with people from a range of cultural origins.

Activity Steps

1. Familiarize yourself with the diagram entitled Cultural Discrepancy Worksheet—Example before proceeding with this activity (see page 143). That sample worksheet and the blank Cultural Discrepancy Worksheet that follows it will help you when you do this activity with clients.

2. Using the sample worksheet as a guide, on a separate sheet of paper or a board, draw three boxes labeled "Culture of Origin," "Cultural Conflict," and "New Culture (USA)."

3. Write "Traits of Culture" below the Culture of Origin box and draw a horizontal arrow alongside it, as shown.

4. Engage the client by asking him what traits define his culture; then write his responses below the Traits of Culture label.

5. Summarize the client's responses. For example, the client might mention language, traditions, and food.

6. Go through the list of Traits of Culture one by one, asking the client how each characteristic he listed compares with those of the new culture. Traditions in the culture of origin may differ from traditions in the new culture.

7. As the client identifies the differences for each trait, visually demonstrate the discrepancies the client sees between the culture of origin and the new culture by placing a hash mark for each discrepancy on the line following Traits of Culture, using the diagram as a guide. Continue until all the discrepancies within the cultural characteristics are addressed. The hash marks should cover the line between the two ends.

8. Ask the client to look at the line and the hash marks, pointing out that he identified numerous cultural discrepancies, and ask if he would like to take a closer look at what these discrepancies might mean to him.

Duplicating this page is illegal. Do not copy this material without written permission from the publisher.

141

9. Ask the client what kind of feelings he has when he experiences discrepancies like the ones he described. Using the diagram on page 143 as a guide, write "Feelings" in the middle of the page or board.

10. List the client's responses under Feelings as he reports them.

11. Ask the client to consider the behaviors those feelings caused. To the right of the client's feelings, list the behaviors he identified. Likely examples of behaviors are joining gangs, using alcohol or drugs, trying to get back at the dominant culture, getting revenge, blaming others, and rejecting more positive values.

12. Ask the client to consider the outcomes of those behaviors and whether they were or were not constructive.

13. Summarize the connection between the behaviors the client has identified and his feelings related to the concept of cultural discrepancies. For example, people who live in a culture different from their culture of origin often feel they don't belong. Joining a gang helps give them a sense of belonging to something.

14. Explore with the client how his drug use conflicts with his understanding of his culture of origin's values, norms, and expectations. For example, if his culture of origin values family relationships, his drug use will most likely cause family conflicts.

15. Point out to the client that it is possible to integrate into the dominant culture without abandoning his culture of origin and that he can do so without using destructive behaviors or feelings as a reaction to the pain caused by cultural discrepancies and uncertainties.

16. Define *assimilation* and *acculturation*. Point out that acculturation is a realistic option.

17. Discuss what it would be like to have a positive bicultural identity.

18. Ask the client how a positive bicultural identity would help him make sense of the cultural discrepancies he sees and experiences.

Cultural Discrepancy Worksheet — Example

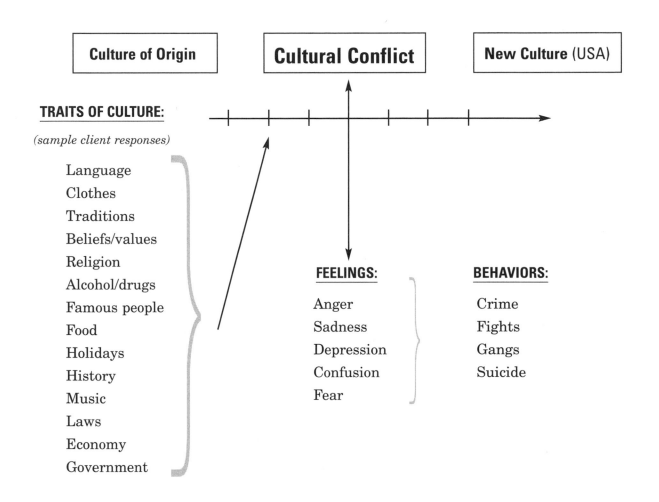

| Culture of Origin | Cultural Conflict | New Culture (USA) |

TRAITS OF CULTURE:

(sample client responses)

Language
Clothes
Traditions
Beliefs/values
Religion
Alcohol/drugs
Famous people
Food
Holidays
History
Music
Laws
Economy
Government

FEELINGS:

Anger
Sadness
Depression
Confusion
Fear

BEHAVIORS:

Crime
Fights
Gangs
Suicide

Define: ASSIMILATION
Define: ACCULTURATION

POSITIVE BICULTURAL IDENTITY

Counselors who work with clients from other cultures should consider developing visuals appropriate to them, such as a Medicine Wheel for Native Americans.

Cultural Discrepancy Worksheet

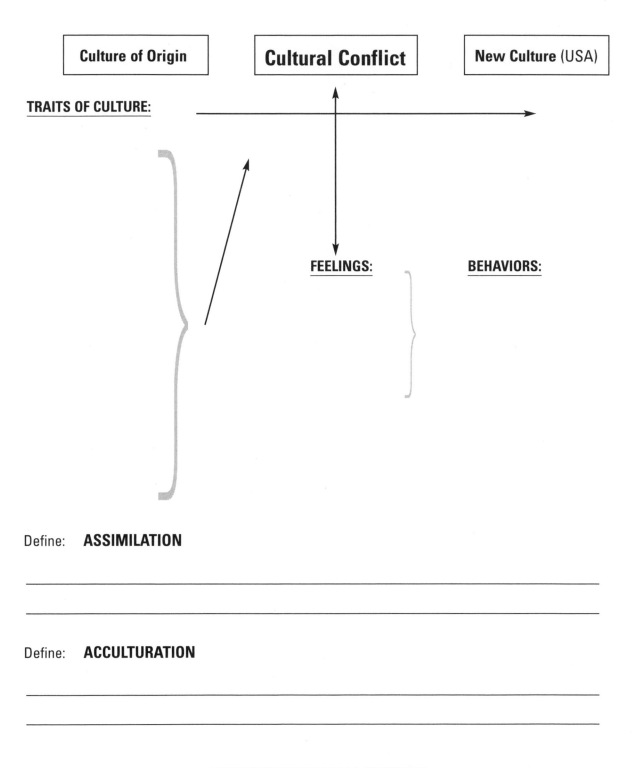

Culture of Origin	Cultural Conflict	New Culture (USA)

TRAITS OF CULTURE:

FEELINGS: **BEHAVIORS:**

Define: **ASSIMILATION**

_____

_____

Define: **ACCULTURATION**

_____

_____

POSITIVE BICULTURAL IDENTITY

Activity Application

1. The conflict between the values of the cultural group you work with and the dominant culture is one of the keys to this exercise, as is the concept of a positive bicultural identification. Helping clients connect drug use to their desire to fit in or their misunderstanding of their culture of origin, and encouraging them to see that their behavior is in conflict with their own cultural values, beliefs, and traditions, is important to developing discrepancy.

2. Through increasing their awareness of cultural discrepancies and engaging them in discussion that affirms their reality while also offering some solutions and perspectives, you support the side of their ambivalence that wants to change. Frequently, clients fail to realize that some of the decisions they have made were in reaction to feelings of anger, sadness, rage, or loneliness. It is imperative to affirm those feelings and normalize them so that clients can begin to make change talk statements as they explore and evaluate the situations that led them to an alcohol- or drug-using pattern or lifestyle.

3. When you summarize the relationships between the client's perception of cultural discrepancies, his feelings, his behaviors, and the outcomes of those behaviors, you help him recognize the roles they play in his poor decisions about using. Your intervention is aimed at helping him reframe his resistance to acculturation by empowering him to define how he wants to live with the dominant culture. The outcome is a client who feels empowered and excited about himself and the options that are open to him.

4. When working with adolescents of diverse cultures, it is helpful for them to recognize that their experiences with cultural conflict are not so different from those of their parents or others who came to this country without even knowing the language. It is also important to get them to see that the clashes they have with their parents about ways in which they want to behave like American kids may be an element of cultural conflict or discrepancy.

Activity 2:

Developing a Positive Cultural Identity

SOC:	Precontemplation
POC:	Consciousness raising
MI Strategies:	Maintain MI style; build rapport and trust; engage client; remain client-centered; monitor resistance; be sensitive to cultural issues; use language appropriate to client experiences and comprehension
MI Skills:	Monitor tone of voice, gestures; use OARS; elicit client concerns; avoid traps
Appropriate for:	Individual session; can be modified for group or family session

Purpose

The activity could be subtitled Enhancing Cultural Self-Efficacy since its purpose is to empower culturally diverse clients to make healthier choices for their future. It is a way of assisting them to increase a positive sense of self culturally and build hope for their future.

Introduction

This activity can be used in conjunction with or separately from the Working through Cultural Discrepancies activity.

Here, the metaphor of a house and its foundation is used to illustrate aspects of clients' lives and to elicit elements of their sense of self. It helps them understand how the effects of substance use can create a shaky foundation. With increased awareness of themselves in five domains—physical, social, mental, emotional, and cultural/spiritual—clients can learn to build a house, or a life, that represents who they truly are or want to be. As they are able to see themselves accurately, they are more able to develop future goals based on a positive cultural sense of self.

The diagram on page 149 is an important part of this activity. We suggest that you change the English terminology to a language appropriate for the client population you work with.

Activity Steps

1. Identify the five common areas of an individual's life—physical, social, mental, emotional, and cultural/spiritual.

2. Using the metaphor of a house for the individual (see the diagram on page 149), define the five areas in the following way:

    a. The cultural/spiritual part of the house is the foundation. The client's foundation is her spirit, the essence of who she is and what she thinks about herself and her cultural background.

    b. The physical room of the house is her health.

    c. The social room is made up of people she considers friends, leisure pursuits, hobbies, and the like.

    d. The mental room is composed of her beliefs.

    e. The emotional room is made up of her values.

3. Go through each room of this house, asking the client what she understands the room to represent in general and how it relates to her personally.

4. Beginning with the physical room, ask the client to identify how each room of her house, other than the foundation, has been affected by her use of substances.

5. Summarize the client's responses, emphasizing the change talk statements made. Remember the value of eliciting desires, abilities, reasons, and needs change talk and their role in increasing strong commitment change talk.

6. Next, ask the client what she thinks the purpose is of the foundation of a house.

7. Point out that using alcohol and drugs affects the foundation of her house. Discuss the possibility that substance abuse might have resulted in her foundation being unstable.

8. Invite the client to explore creating a more complete foundation for her house. (Because of earlier rapport building, clients rarely refuse this invitation.)

9. Explain that the foundation of the house is where cultural and spiritual beliefs, experiences, and hopes lie. Ask the client to consider the foundation as the essence of who she is.

10. Ask the client to describe spirituality. The client responds. Remember to reflect, support, and so on.

11. Ask permission to share what others in the client's situation have discovered, such as ways they have empowered themselves to make different choices based on an increased awareness of their culture. Invite the client to explore what she would like to learn most regarding her cultural and spiritual identity, history, values, customs, religious beliefs, and so on. (See the note on page 149 related to adolescents.)

12. Help the client see that part of her treatment-planning process in this program is building a stronger foundation. Encourage hope by exploring activities for the client to learn about her culture, perhaps by conducting research via the Internet or the library, talking to family members, attending cultural community events, or finding a mentor from her culture of origin.

13. Depending on the client's readiness, develop either an awareness plan or an action plan with which she can explore and work out who she is as a bicultural person.

Activity Application

1. Keep in mind that you communicate how important it is for clients to establish a sense of self from a cultural perspective. If you do not believe this is of value or marginalize its importance, your clients will not be convinced that their cultural identity is valuable. Building hope and empowerment through enhancing self-esteem is essential for culturally diverse clients who have lost their sense of who they are separate from substances, especially if their substance abuse is severe.

2. Attending to clients and listening well is essential. Allow yourself to learn from them as you guide them during this process of discovery. A true sense of collaboration is conveyed in your interactions with your clients during the course of this and subsequent sessions.

Note: When working with adolescents, address developmental issues that relate to the connection between cultural identity and self-identity. Relevant issues include relationships with peers, comparing their lives to those of their families of origin, discovering who they are in relationship to the opposite sex, and so on.

Creating a Positive Cultural Identity

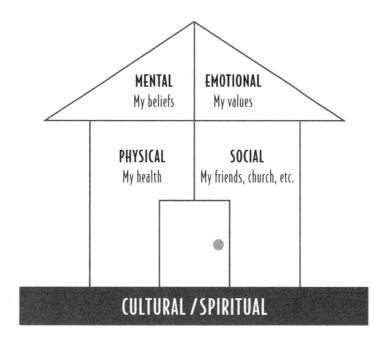

Case Study of a Client with a Co-occurring Disorder

As we mentioned earlier, engagement is crucial in working with clients who have co-occurring disorders. We present a case study here rather than activities in order to illustrate how to motivate into treatment a client with co-occurring disorders, in this case, a person with an alcohol problem and depression. This case study is not drawn from real life, but it is reflective of real clients in real circumstances.

In this case study, we describe a man with substance abuse co-occurring with depression. Following this description is a script of the dialogue between him and his therapist. Notice how the therapist uses principles similar to the ones discussed previously in this book. Here they are used primarily to engage the client and keep him coming back for ongoing assessment, rapport building, and establishment of trust. These must occur in order to move toward the therapist's goals of getting the patient on appropriate medication and examining how his alcohol use relates to his symptoms of depression. Here is a brief description of the client.

> Henry is a forty-seven-year-old married male who presents identifying himself as both Caucasian and Native American. He comes to treatment due to family pressures. He currently lives at home; however, his recent descent into severe symptoms of depression and his regular use of alcohol has led to a reduction of his ability to function at home. At times, Henry has not been able to get out of bed, often spending days sleeping and not eating. Generally, when he does get up, he drinks up to a pint of whiskey at any one time. Henry does not believe he has an alcohol or drug problem. He knows that he gets depressed but believes he can handle it on his own, as he has many times in the past. He came to this treatment appointment only because his wife threatened to kick him out of the house.

The script, or communication, between Henry and his counselor appears on pages 151–54. The parenthetical comments relate to the counselor's behavior and statements.

Counselor: Hello Henry. My name is Gloria. (Tries to engage.)

Client: *No response.*

Counselor: I am wondering, what brings you here today? (Asks an open-ended question.)

Client: *Pause.* I don't know—I guess my wife thought it would be a good idea.

Counselor: Tell me what concerns your wife has shared with you that led you to come in today. (Focus on concerns of others is a strategy for eliciting change talk. Asks for more information and elaboration.)

Client: She thinks I have a problem with drinking, which I DO NOT!

Counselor: One of her concerns is that she thinks your drinking is a problem, and you definitely disagree with that concern. What else has she shared with you? (Asks for elaboration.)

Client: Well, she thinks I sleep too much. I know I have been down a bit, but I have always been able to take care of this on my own. I don't need help.

Counselor: In the past, when you have experienced problems like depression or feeling down, you *have* handled it on your own. Sounds like you feel some pressure to be here, and you think she is overreacting. (Affirms, reflects.)

Client: Yeah. I know I have been sleeping a lot, and sometimes that has worried me, but I am not crazy. I just need a little time to get back on my feet, that's all.

Counselor: So you acknowledge that your sleeping has been more than in the past, but you think time will take care of that, and you will be able to get back to normal. (Reflects.)

Client: Yeah—I am not crazy.

Counselor: Another concern you have is that if you need help, people might think you are crazy. (Reflects.)

Client: Yeah, I guess so. I don't think it is that bad, really.

Counselor: Coming to a place like this may imply to you and others that you cannot handle your own life. (Reflects.)

Client: Well, isn't that what people believe?

Counselor: I can see that what others think about your coming to counseling or to a "shrink" may indeed seem strange and unnecessary to you. You may have wondered yourself if you are crazy for even being here now. (Reflects.)

Client: Well, am I right?

Counselor: Sometimes other people that I have seen in situations similar to yours have told me the same thing. They are worried about being seen as crazy, worried about what that means, and worried about how others may treat them. What I will tell you is that there is help available to manage your depression so that you don't sleep so much and so you feel more like your old self. I also know that when people do take advantage of treatment, they often tell me that things got better for them. But I think it is up to you to decide if this is something you want to look into. Since you did take the time to come in here today, I am wondering if you would like to get more information about the treatment choices that are available before you make your decision about what you think is best for you. (Affirms and uses the experience of others to avoid appearing to be the expert, avoids labeling, stays with the client. Offers information, reduces resistance, empowers.)

Client: Now that you put it that way, that I have choices, I guess it won't hurt me to hear what you have to say. I am not making any promises.

Counselor: Okay. Let me go over some of the options available to you. (Counselor presents options available related to medication, information about the program including treatment groups to manage depression symptoms, information about how the use of alcohol contributes to depression symptoms, and so on. Appropriateness of options presented requires assessing propensity for suicide, the ability to function on an outpatient basis, and the like.)

Counselor: What do you think about the options available to you? (Offers information, asks an open-ended question, asks for thoughts from the client about the next step.)

Client: I don't know if I want drugs. I have heard there are some really bad side effects to those. I would be willing to discuss how to manage my depression without sleeping so much. If I could just feel normal again, like wanting to get up, that would help. Maybe I can just come in and see you for a couple of times.

Counselor: You have heard that certain treatments for depression, like medication, are not helpful. You also are not sure about group involvement, but you may want to come and discuss with me how to help you get up and moving around more. (Reflects.)

Client: Yeah! You know my wife thinks I need drugs. I took them before, but I hate relying on something like that.

Counselor: Tell me what your experiences have been when you have taken medications for depression. (Counselor narrows to concern about medications, gathering more data about the client's experiences.)

Client: They did seem to help, but I lost my sexual drive, got too lethargic, and gained some weight, so I stopped. (Counselor continues to explore medication experiences, including whether Henry was being medically monitored and by

Duplicating this page is illegal. Do not copy this material without written permission from the publisher.

153

whom, whether he expressed concerns to his provider about negative side effects, how long he took his medications and what types.)

Counselor: It sounds like you made an effort to follow the advice of your prescribing physician, but you did not let her know that you were having problems with side effects. (Summarizes and builds discrepancy. Respects client's readiness for change.)

Client: Yeah—I know my wife is going to want me back on them. I just know it.

Counselor: Well, what do you think would be helpful? (Empowers client to make the decision.)

Client: I would reconsider looking into it, but I will not keep taking them if I continue to have problems.

Counselor: Sounds like you are prepared to try the medications again, but they will need to work better for you if you stay on them. (Reflects and reframes the client's concerns.)

Client: You got it!

Counselor: I heard you mention earlier that coming in to talk with me would be all right with you. Tell me how that would be helpful to you. (Elicits change talk, reinforces client decisions, and reflects.)

The counselor continues the session, concluding with a summary of the key points, including recapping the client's change talk statements and making the next appointment. Notice that the counselor avoids, for the most part, the client's resistance to discussing his use of alcohol. The tactic is to follow the client's lead in order to retain him in counseling. Building a positive rapport and gaining trust are necessary before the counselor can broach a topic that is likely to generate anxiety in the client.

Closing Remarks

In this chapter, we have presented approaches to working with special populations that honor clients' unique characteristics and are consistent with the principles of MI and the process of change. Over time, your client population will probably include members of special populations other than the three we address here. The key points to remember in approaching clients from special populations remain the same. Focus on engagement. Know each population's unique characteristics. Work collaboratively with clients and be mindful of your role as a guide of *their* process.

In the final chapter, we address special issues and concerns for counselors and the realities of their work life in implementing a "best practice." This requires innovation and determination on the part of those who serve clients. It also requires that counselors and other agency staff examine their own issues about changing their view of counseling and the services the agency is providing. We encourage you, as the reader—whether counselor, supervisor, or manager—to seriously consider these challenges.

■ ■ ■

Duplicating this page is illegal. Do not copy this material without written permission from the publisher.

155

PUTTING MOTIVATIONAL INTERVIEWING AND STAGES OF CHANGE INTO PRACTICE

Everything is connected . . . no one thing can change by itself.

— PAUL HAWKE

Thus far, we have discussed the research supporting Motivational Interviewing and Stages of Change, provided a brief description of both approaches, and outlined the way in which we have blended them in the practice of counseling substance-abusing clients. We have also introduced a number of activities for you to use with your clients as you explore this material. By now you have had a chance to consider whether or not the counseling method and style presented in this book is right for you. Some of you will be excited by the material and strive to integrate it into your practice. Others will use some portions of the information and not others. In this chapter, we offer some final thoughts and tools to help you continue to work with the material on your own or within an organization.

As well you may know from your work with clients, change does not come easily. Even though the possibility of improving your practice and client outcomes is exciting, the pull of the familiar, the tried and true, is strong. This is true for organizations as well as individuals. Most likely you work within the context of an organization that has an existing philosophy and culture. You are accountable to various forces. The people you work with and for have their own attitudes and beliefs about appropriate and acceptable counseling practices and outcomes. The larger political and social environment may place limitations on and have expectations of what you can accomplish and how you should go about doing it. Wherever you work, the surrounding environment affects how you practice your craft.

Duplicating this page is illegal. Do not copy this material without written permission from the publisher.

157

In the best of circumstances, change takes time and persistence. A heavy workload can leave you with little or no time to learn and apply new material. If you are alone in your desire to make changes, isolation can be wearing and may lead you to give up trying. Opposition from colleagues who don't want to change what they are doing can effectively sabotage your efforts. Other obstacles may arise. Clearly you need support. If at all possible, find a supervisor who is knowledgeable about MI and SOC. If you have a supervisor who is not familiar with this material, your enthusiasm for it can pique her interest and support. Searching out colleagues who are interested in trying new approaches will enhance your continuing success. Keep learning and practicing; build on what you already know.

While there are predictable challenges to trying something new, program managers and staff usually are interested in anything that will improve outcomes for their clients. Their dilemma revolves around introducing new technologies in a manner that recognizes the many issues that are bound to arise, while at the same time creating a receptive, participatory audience. The issues include acknowledging the reality of financial impact; respecting the effectiveness of current practices; understanding counselors' possible fears of inadequacy at mastering new techniques; being sensitive to application to clients of varying ages, cultures, genders, family makeup, and so on; and listening effectively to the concerns and needs of counselors and their clients.

We submit for your consideration samples of materials and tools you can use as you contemplate the challenges that often exist when implementing best practices such as Motivational Interviewing and Stages of Change. The materials and tools presented in this chapter are designed primarily to help the practicing clinician work with MI and SOC. A section that addresses application of the tool in a counseling or agency setting follows each tool. Additional materials that facilitate brief reviews of basic MI and SOC terms and ideas, and are useful during counseling sessions, are included in appendix A. Appendix B contains materials related to larger agency issues that occur in the process of implementing new practices in an existing organization.

The tools that follow are a Guide to MI/SOC Case Presentation Format, a Staff Readiness for Change form, examples of MI and SOC rating forms, and an example of an MI/SOC Treatment Plan that includes sample documentation. For counselors who use the American Society of Addiction Medicine (ASAM)

Patient Placement II-R[1] format, this case presentation format is consistent with the theory and practice of ASAM, especially as it relates to Dimension IV Readiness for Change. For those who do not use a patient placement format such as ASAM, the case presentation tool is a suggested format to guide your thinking about clients' readiness for change and ways of addressing identified treatment needs using the theory, skills, and strategies suggested in an MI/SOC model.

Guide to MI/SOC Case Presentation

When experimenting with counseling approaches such as MI and SOC, we often are confronted with concerns about how competent we feel in our ability to integrate new information into our existing work style. One way of addressing these feelings involves using the following case presentation format, which is based on the concepts of MI/SOC. Using this approach to present cases to peers or supervisors in your organization will give you an opportunity to apply these concepts in a practical setting. It can guide you through the steps of a case presentation, keeping you focused on important elements of MI/SOC and giving you a chance to develop comfort and skill with what is new to you.

GUIDE TO MI/SOC CASE PRESENTATION FORMAT

When working in a clinical setting, applying the concepts of Motivational Interviewing and Stages of Change can be confusing, especially if your program design has not adjusted to these ideas and beliefs. However, it is still possible to introduce MI/SOC into your work with clients. This format is designed to help you present clinical cases from a MI/SOC perspective. It can be used as a guide to begin discussions about implementation strategies and clinical strengths, which can lead to improvements in clinical practice and programming.

    I. Client identifying information

        1. Present the client case by identifying the following: Name, cultural background, age, gender, family status (including marital status and children)

        2. Describe what brought the client into treatment

3. If the client is an adolescent or young adult, describe developmental issues that may apply

4. Include any other information the counselor considers significant to report

II. Readiness for change and stage identification

1. Describe the client's readiness for change

2. What are the client's internal motivators for change?

III. Motivational counseling style and strategies

1. Describe the counselor's relationship with the client

2. Has an atmosphere been established that is conducive to change? (yes/no)

   a. If yes, please describe

   b. If no, what are the issues that prevent this from happening?

3. What are some strategies to resolve the issues identified?

4. Has the counselor considered the client's ambivalence in relationship to any perceived resistance?

5. Based on the presentation, what are the next steps to be taken with this client?

Application

Prior to presenting a case

1. Be prepared. Review the case before presenting it so that you can focus on the MI/SOC elements you wish to include.

2. Keep it simple. Take only a minute or two to present the information in the first section. Its purpose is to acquaint the listeners with basic information about the client's situation.

3. Assess readiness. It is important to explore readiness before attempting to apply MI interventions and skills. Before you can intervene effectively, you need to know your client's stage of change so that the strategies you are considering using are appropriate.

4. Apply the MI strategies. Section III on the case presentation format is where you apply the MI beliefs to the case presentation. Notice that we continue to emphasize the importance of your relationship with your client as being fundamental to the application of MI strategies.

Staff Readiness for Change Form

Once you have presented a few cases in this manner, and perhaps have received feedback and comments from others, you might wonder how ready you really are to change the way you work with clients. One way to explore this question is to evaluate your own readiness to change. The Staff Readiness for Change form on page 163 can help you do that. It is based on the concepts of MI/SOC and serves as a way of determining how prepared staff are to implement new practices into their work within the context of the agency that employs them. Keep in mind that even the person who is highly motivated to change is affected by his or her environment.

Duplicating this page is illegal. Do not copy this material without written permission from the publisher.

161

Application

1. After taking this assessment, repeat it in a month or two. You may find your assessment of your readiness and confidence changes over time. You may also find that you will need others in your agency to change with you in order for you to be fully effective.

2. Responding to this tool may lead you to contemplate the attitude of your workplace toward making change and consider discussing the changes you wish to make with your immediate managers and/or supervisors. Getting their support is important for you to progress since change takes time and effort, and it is easy to get caught up in other requirements. Having a concrete tool such as this assessment form can give you a way to talk with them about your goals for your professional development.

3. Engage other co-workers in their own self-assessments. As you progress in changing your practice, having a peer to talk with is helpful and reinforces what you are trying to accomplish not only for yourself, but for them as well.

Staff Readiness for Change

1. I am open to implementing MI/SOC and other research-based practices.

1	2	3	4	5
not at all	very little	somewhat	mostly	very much

2. I am fully trained in the practice of MI/SOC.

1	2	3	4	5
not at all	very little	somewhat	mostly	very much

3. The agency I work in can support me in providing these kinds of services.

1	2	3	4	5
not at all	very little	somewhat	mostly	very much

4. People in my program trust each other enough to submit samples of their work for review and/or role-play case scenarios for feedback and professional growth.

1	2	3	4	5
not at all	very little	somewhat	mostly	very much

5. I have the confidence to improve my skills using MI/SOC.

1	2	3	4	5
not at all	very little	somewhat	mostly	very much

6. The staff in my agency is under too much pressure to implement MI/SOC or other best practices at this time.

1	2	3	4	5
not at all	very little	somewhat	mostly	very much

7. Upper-level management will support staff improvements for professional growth.

1	2	3	4	5
not at all	very little	somewhat	mostly	very much

continued on other side

Now that you have considered the issues involved with implementing MI/SOC within your practice, list those areas in which you feel strong and those areas you need to improve.

Areas of Strength

1. _____

2. _____

3. _____

Areas for Improvement

1. _____

2. _____

3. _____

MI and SOC Rating Forms

Thus far, the tools we have offered to help you apply MI/SOC to your practice are a case presentation format and a readiness for change form, with which you can assess your readiness to incorporate these concepts. Another aspect of this process to consider is the development of specific skills basic to MI. The use of rating sheets can help you evaluate your progress in acquiring these skills.

Four examples of rating sheets follow, each focused on Phase 1 skills or traps to avoid. They are entitled (1) Open-Ended Questions, Closed-Ended Questions, and Reflections; (2) Levels of Reflection; (3) Affirmations and Summaries; and (4) Exploration of Phase 1 Traps. Following the rating sheets themselves are suggestions for their use (see Application section).

The rating sheet format can be used to develop additional forms to explore other skills you are interested in enhancing. These tools were developed for application in clinical settings and should not be used for performance appraisal purposes. They are intended to assess and guide the progress of counselors interested in acquiring these skills. Audio- or videotapes can be used, or an actual session may be observed. Evaluation can be done through self-assessment, peer assessment, or in a supervision session.

MI PHASE 1:
Open-Ended Questions, Closed-Ended Questions, and Reflections

Self/Peer/Supervisor Rating Form

1. # _____ **Open-ended questions**

   An open-ended question is designed to elicit information, which requires a response from the client that is more than yes, no, or a brief phrase. Effective use of open-ended questions assists the client and counselor to engage in client-centered interactions, which allows for exploration of client concerns, hopes, and feelings.

   Examples:

   _____

   _____

   _____

   _____

   _____

2. # _____ **Closed-ended questions**

   Closed-ended questions can be answered with yes, no, or a brief response.

   Examples:

   _____

   _____

   _____

   _____

   _____

continued on other side

3. # _____ **Reflections**

   Reflections are statements rather than questions. Reflections communicate to the client that he or she has been heard and understood.

   Examples:

   _____

   _____

   _____

   _____

   _____

   _____

TRAPS:

Question/answer: _____

Expert: _____

Blaming: _____

Taking a side: _____

Labeling: _____

Premature focus: _____

MI PHASE 1:
Levels of Reflections

Self/Peer/Supervisor Rating Form

Reflections

Reflections are statements rather than questions. Reflections communicate to the client that he or she has been heard and understood.

LEVEL 1: # _____

Extent to which counselor repeated (using exact words) what the client was saying.

Examples:

_____

_____

_____

_____

_____

LEVEL 2: # _____

Extent to which counselor rephrased (slight rewording) what the client was saying.

Examples:

_____

_____

_____

_____

_____

continued on other side

LEVEL 3: # _____

Extent to which counselor paraphrased (inferred meaning, reflected feelings, used analogies and metaphors, offered empathy) what the client was saying.

Examples:

_____

_____

_____

_____

_____

TRAPS:

Question/answer: _____

Expert: _____

Blaming: _____

Taking a side: _____

Labeling: _____

Premature focus: _____

MI PHASE 1:
Affirmations and Summaries

Self/Peer/Supervisor Rating Form

1. **# _____ Affirmations**

   Affirmations are statements of appreciation and acknowledgment of the client's strengths, talents, and skills. Affirmations can encourage the development of self-efficacy within the client. Using affirmations is another way to let clients know you hear and appreciate their efforts toward change.

   Examples:

   _____

   _____

   _____

   _____

   _____

2. **# _____ Summaries**

   Summaries are forms of reflection that highlight the main points of the counselor-client interaction. Using summaries allows the clinician to direct clients toward moving in the change process and provides information for clients while they go through this process. A counselor can conduct mini-summaries, session summaries, and transitional summaries.

   Examples:

   _____

   _____

   _____

   _____

   _____

continued on other side

TRAPS:

Question/answer: _____

Expert: _____

Blaming: _____

Taking a side: _____

Labeling: _____

Premature focus: _____

Exploration of Phase 1 Traps

Self/Peer/Supervisor Rating Form

QUESTION/ANSWER: # _____

Following one question with another and another without reflections.

Examples:

_____

_____

_____

EXPERT: # _____

In interactions with a client, taking the position that you know what is best for the client, even if the client does not agree with your assessment.

Examples:

_____

_____

_____

BLAMING: # _____

Blaming clients when they do not follow your suggestions. Taking an "I am right, you are not" position, especially in the earlier phases of change.

Examples:

_____

_____

_____

continued on other side

TAKING A SIDE: # _____

Taking the side of change, inadvertently reinforcing clients' ambivalence and resistance toward change.

Examples:

_____

_____

_____

LABELING: # _____

Labeling clients limits them as people. Examples of labels include addict, alcoholic, precontemplator, contemplator, *and so on.*

Examples:

_____

_____

_____

PREMATURE FOCUS: # _____

Assuming and acting as if clients are more ready for change than they are and then intervening in a manner that is ahead of them in the change process.

Examples:

_____

_____

_____

Eliciting Change Talk: Part A

CATEGORIES	EXAMPLES	REINFORCED YES NO	STRENGTH OF COMMITMENT LOW HIGH 1 2 3
Desires			
Abilities			
Reasons			
Needs			

Counselor Demonstrated Methods of Eliciting Change Talk: Part B

Methods	Yes	No	Client Response
Asking Evocative Questions			
Using Importance/ Confidence Ruler			
Creating a Decisional Balance			
Asking for Elaboration			
Questioning Extremes			
Looking Forward/ Looking Back			
Exploring Goals and Values			

Application

1. There are several ways to use these rating sheets to evaluate the acquisition and integration of MI skills and strategies.

   a. One method is to use them during a live session in which you are observed by a colleague or supervisor. Choose a rating sheet that focuses on a skill you wish to work on, such as the use of open-ended questions. Ask your peer or supervisor to complete the form, including examples. There is an area on the form to count certain skills. Counting the skills is helpful when assessing whether or not the skill is used strategically. For example, the number of open-ended questions to closed-ended questions should equal a ratio of about 2:3, or the number of open-ended questions to reflections should equal 1:3. Monitoring the strategic use of skills used is important to determine the overall effectiveness of motivational interventions made. Finally, arrange a time to review the form with the person who rated you, ideally close to when the session occurred, if not right afterward.

   b. A second method is to make an audio- or videotape of a session. Many times clients may feel uneasy in their session during audio- or video-taping. It is important to address their fears, concerns, or anxiety by explaining how the tape will be used, who will see or hear the tape, and if they will be identified in any way. In many agencies, permission must be obtained from the client before taping can take place. Please address these concerns directly with your clients and follow all protocols expected where you practice. You can review the tape using a rating sheet of your choice. You may do this alone or with others.

   c. A third method is to review the work of a colleague. While you are using the rating form, you can remind yourself of the meaning and use of the terms while you observe how someone else applies the material to work similar to your own.

   d. Another method is to focus on the Exploration of Phase 1 Traps sheet. This sheet examines "what not to do" rather than "what to do." After completing this sheet, determine what you can do to improve your practice.

2. It is important to use the rating sheets in the context of a learning environment, one that is nonjudgmental and acknowledges that learning new skills takes time and necessarily involves making mistakes. Maintaining a sense that "we are all in this together" helps reduce the anxiety you and others may experience when experimenting with new skills.

3. You can develop rating sheets for your own purposes. For example, creating a rating sheet focused on change talk requires you to review the meaning and goals of this strategy. It also inspires you to consider ways to improve the use of this strategy in your work.

4. A cautionary note: It is important to get feedback from others. You may be doing well in skill acquisition but not notice that you have inadvertently fallen into traps or a practice that is not consistent with the application of MI. The most common areas of concern involve the question/answer trap and getting ahead of clients in the wish for them to change. A rating sheet with feedback from others can help you become aware of and avoid these problems.

MI/SOC Treatment Plan

This final tool will help you practice writing and documenting a treatment plan using MI/SOC. On pages 180–82, you'll find a sample MI/SOC treatment plan. Treatment planning for clients using the ideas and concepts of MI/SOC can be challenging. In many programs, treatment is seen as a succession of groups in which individual contact with clients is limited. This approach often is based on the assumption that clients are motivated to change and ignores the need to explore their thoughts, feelings, and ambivalence about their substance use. Even in organizations that support the MI/SOC approach, treatment planning can baffle the most skilled counselors. As outcomes become a priority for programs, individualizing client treatment and treatment planning receives greater emphasis. Frequently, that means struggling with standardized services that do not readily lend themselves to individualization of care. The sample treatment plan that follows is offered to guide your thinking about how treatment plans can be adapted to program settings as treatment programs strive to individualize care. If your agency already provides high-quality individualized care, this example may help you continue to improve care to your clients.

A series of tips for treatment planning follows the sample plan. Several of the activities proposed in earlier chapters are useful in relationship to the tips. For example, the activity Developing a Change Plan in chapter 4 is useful with tip 3, which addresses redefining the treatment plan. Collaborating for Choices in chapter 3, which describes how to establish client-centered treatment goals, can be useful in relation to several of the tips.

It is possible to create treatment plans using the concepts of MI/SOC. Thinking about how clients change, where they are in the process of change, and what will move them toward achieving their goals all can be part of a client-centered treatment plan. This approach allows the treatment planning process to be a client-centered and meaningful activity for clients and clinicians. The sample plan can assist you in becoming proficient at writing MI/SOC-based treatment plans.

Sample MI/SOC Treatment Plan

The following treatment plan format includes a client-generated problem statement and the identification of client strengths, followed by goals for treatment and methods, or strategies, to attain the identified goals. It also contains a quick, easy method of documenting progress on goals and objectives. This treatment plan example is generic and can be adapted to your agency standards.

Treatment Planning and Documentation Example

Client Problem Statement: "I'd like to get my probation officer off my back and get out of the legal system so that I can have my life back."	**Client Strengths:** 1. Client working 2. Good verbal skills 3. Some insight 4. Some motivation

Client Goal: **Date Identified: 3/7**

The client knows that he is required to remain free from use of all substances; he is not sure he needs to, but he will to finish probation. The client stated that on occasion he knows that some of his friendships and activities led to drinking more than he intended. He would like to keep his friends while also making new friends who drink less.

Strategies to Meet Goals:

1. Complete a decisional balance sheet about using friends.
   (Client strength: 3)

2. Discuss ways to incorporate new friendships while keeping those friends who he thinks will support his treatment.
   (Client strengths: 2, 3, 4)

Progress:

Date: 3/20

In the last few weeks, the client reported some progress in making new friends. He found that not all people need to use.

Date: 3/27

The client decided to go to a party with old friends and did not find it as much fun. Client vowed to find new friends by joining a bowling league.

Date: 4/14

Client joined bowling league from work. He found new people he liked both at work and in the bowling league.

Date: 4/24

Client asked old friends to help him stay away from using while with them. Friends agreed to help, which surprised the client. Client felt he had more support should he decide not to drink while completing probation.

Client Goal: **Date Identified: 3/7**

Stop using while in treatment. Client states he can stop drinking while he is on probation and to complete treatment. He has not decided if this change will go beyond treatment.

Strategies to Meet Goals:

1. Explore reasons why client would continue to use and why client would stop using.
   (Client strengths: 2, 3, 4)

2. Ask client to consider his life a few years from now. How would his use fit in, and what would it be like for him in the future?
   (Client strengths: 1, 2, 3, 4)

3. Continue to monitor client's motivation and confidence around staying clean.
   (Client strength: 4)

Progress:

Date: 3/14

Client reported no use. He stated it was not a problem and he feels great.

Date: 3/28

Client experienced a lot of triggers to use while hanging around old friends. Initially, he thought he could keep his friends, but now he is reconsidering. He is still committed to staying clean.

Date: 4/4

Client knows that he needs to stay clean to get out of legal problems but wonders if he needs to abstain long term. Client and this counselor agreed to continue to discuss his thoughts and plans regarding ongoing use after treatment. Client stated he felt glad he could talk honestly about his use.

Date: 4/24

Client is able to stay clean and is surprised to find out his old "using" friends were actually more supportive to assist him in maintaining abstinence. As a result of this experience, the client seems more motivated to reconsider his use beyond probation and treatment for social and family reasons.

Client Goal: **Date Identified: 3/7**

"Get my family life back." Despite his using problems, the client states that he and his family members have been in conflict about his trouble with the law. They know that at times he drinks too much, but they want him to get his life organized and stay out of legal trouble. They want fewer conflicts at home and better communication. Client wants to establish better family life.

Strategies to Meet Goals:

1. Complete a values worksheet about family life. Have client describe family values lost due to recent legal problems and his thoughts about reestablishing the most important values with his family.
   (Client strengths: 1, 2, 3, 4)

2. Invite family members, with client's permission, to share with the client the effect of his legal problems on their family.
   (Client strengths: 3, 4)

3. Present material on skills related to family communication and ask family to practice skills between meetings.
   (Client strengths: 2, 3)

Progress:

Date: 3/14

First family meeting with client. In attendance were client's spouse and two children. Invited the family to discuss family values using values worksheet. Family was able to be honest with client, and client was able to talk about his needs related to improving family life. Family agreed to continue to discuss and reestablish a values list for next meeting.

Date: 3/28

Family values reviewed. Family stated they are able to communicate, but at times tempers flare. Client openly admits that he is embarrassed with his legal situation and did try to protect his family from his problems, but without much success. Family stated that this approach kept too much distance, resulting in conflicts and tension. All family members would like life at home to be less tense. They agreed to commit to one family activity in the next few weeks and to continue to work on communication.

Date: 4/3

Communication model presented to family on this date. Report from last meeting is that when they go out, it is fun, but at times they bicker with each other needlessly. Family listened to and practiced information about communication skills. Based on recent attempts to reestablish family life, the family was able to see how to use these skills to begin the process of building trust again. Family seemed hopeful about improvements and will continue to practice communicating at home.

Tips for Treatment Planning

1. Define the problem by collaborating with the client, using the client's perspective with counselor input.

2. Decide the client's stage of change related to the problems presented.

3. Engage the client around the development of the treatment plan by redefining it as a *change* plan. Start the change plan with how the treatment services available to the client will help her to accomplish her goals.

4. Highlight and reinforce the client's strengths in the plan.

5. Match the appropriate treatment interventions to the client's stage of change.

6. Monitor and support the client to determine how her plans are working.

7. Assist the client in modifying the plan, if necessary, to improve chances for successful change.

8. If the plan is not working, continue to personalize feedback about the problem area by eliciting change talk while staying client-centered and continuing to assess readiness for change.

9. The client should be able to talk about her change plan to others who are also assisting her in the program, both other clients and counselors.

10. Avoid the trap of getting ahead of the client in the change process.

11. Involve significant others in treatment planning and progress, if appropriate.

12. Tie treatment plans to the values and goals of the client.

13. Remember to monitor successful completion of goals and movement toward maintaining values consistent with change in lifestyle choices.

14. The strategies to meet goals are identified for each problem to help the client and counselor meet their goals for treatment. The strategies would result from a discussion between the client and counselor.

Closing Remarks

The tools in this chapter are practical. They, and the activities from earlier chapters, offer tastes of an exciting, productive way of supporting substance-abusing clients as they reach for recovery. Additional materials that help in reviewing and using the key MI/SOC ideas presented in this book are included in appendix A in the form of an MI/SOC Guide to Practice and At-a-Glance sheets. Appendix A begins with the Guide to Practice and a discussion of how the materials in it can be used by both supervisors and counselors in a variety of ways. The Guide to Practice contains a summary of MI Phase 1 and Phase 2 concepts and traps to avoid. It contains a definition of each stage of change along with counselor goals for each stage and a section that identifies and defines the processes of change. At-a-Glance sheets are included for each of the stages of change. They can be used in sessions with clients. The sheets themselves are preceded by a discussion of their use in practical situations.

The Implementation Plan Development Checklist and Sample Implementation Plan contained in appendix B will enable you to familiarize yourself with elements of organizational change. These documents were created in concert with Susan Hayashi, Ph.D., and Judy Huang, Ph.D., whose research in the field of implementation was the basis for the Implementation Plan Development Checklist; the documents relate to issues that occur when an organization attempts to implement new practices such as MI/SOC within an existing program. It is important to recognize that staff on all levels are affected by the decisions and policies of the agency they work in. If you intend to use this material in your practice, and you work in an organization that has not fully accepted the tenets and methods of MI or SOC, the material contained in this appendix can give you something to consider as you approach the implementation of MI/SOC into your agency. This knowledge may help you be more effective in advocating for and assisting in the change process. Providing feedback on the effect of using MI/SOC with your clients can positively effect change within your agency on many levels. It can demonstrate greater client retention, improve client satisfaction, and assist the manager to provide data for outcomes to support the agency and your practice as well. The plan and checklist can help guide your thinking about the kinds of interventions that would be useful in your workplace.

What we have covered in this book is the proverbial tip of the iceberg. We encourage you to experiment with the activities presented here and try them out as you encounter your clients. The materials we offer to you highlight the strategies and concepts inherent in MI/SOC. We hope that what we have described here will pique your interest and prove to be of value in your ongoing quest to improve your work and serve your clients well.

■ ■ ■

GUIDE TO PRACTICE AND
AT-A-GLANCE SHEETS

This appendix contains a Guide to Practice for MI/SOC, the Processes of Change, and At-a-Glance sheets, which provide a clear summary of the key ideas and language of MI/SOC. The three are useful for both counselors and supervisors. The guide contains specific language that counselors can use to discuss their practice. Supervisors can use it to assist counselors to learn the theories and acquire the skills and strategies of MI/SOC. Listed below are a number of approaches to using the guide for counselors and supervisors.

How Counselors Can Use This Guide

1. This guide can be used to structure discussions with colleagues about the application of the principles of MI/SOC to clients in your caseload. One option is to review the various stages of change to assess whether a particular client fits the description of a specific stage of change. Discussion with other colleagues' interpretations of the same material can be helpful in integrating this material.

2. The practice guide can be taken into a counseling session with clients as a reminder of MI/SOC concepts. It is especially helpful when you need prompting about specific skills and corresponding strategies that apply to a client in a particular stage of change.

3. The guide can help identify traps that you want to avoid as you implement MI/SOC into your counseling approach. Knowing what not to do and having a name for it can be instructive. The guide can help you keep in mind behaviors to avoid while you practice or refine behaviors you are developing or enhancing.

Duplicating this page is illegal. Do not copy this material without written permission from the publisher.

187

How Supervisors Can Use This Guide

1. Reviewing sections of this material in a group supervision setting is a great way to utilize the practice guide. Discussing sections contained in the guide will aid and encourage the staff's learning. Bringing the practice guides to staffings can communicate to your clinical team your expectations about their ongoing development in this arena.

2. Training staff on an ongoing basis is often a supervisory function. Using the practice guide as part of an orientation for new staff will give them information about how you expect them to approach clients and what terminology your organization uses. It can also provide an opportunity to discuss how you can assist them in acquiring needed knowledge or skills.

3. The guide can also be used to help referring personnel understand the way your treatment agency functions with clients. Particularly when an organization changes how it works with or talks about clients, those who make referrals may not be familiar with the latest advances in care. The practice guide can help them learn about and adjust to the new approach.

Guide to Phase 1 Motivational Interviewing Concepts

This guide contains a summary of the main concepts of MI and SOC. For those who are familiar with the information, this guide is an easy-to-use reference for counseling sessions with clients. For those who are learning the concepts, the guide can also be used as an ongoing reference to aid in further integration of the material. In Phase 1, the first four skills use the acronym OARS.[1]

1. **Open-ended questions:** An open-ended question is designed to elicit information, which requires a response from the client that is more than yes, no, or a brief phrase. Effective use of open-ended questions assists the client and counselor to engage in client-centered interactions, which allows for exploration of client concerns, hopes, and feelings.

2. **Closed-ended questions:** Closed-ended questions can be answered with yes, no, or a brief response. This type of question should be used primarily for clarification purposes and only occasionally throughout sessions.

3. **Reflections:** Reflections are statements. They are not questions. Reflections communicate to the client that he or she has been heard and understood.

> Level 1: Counselor repeats (using exact words) what the client says.
>
> Level 2: Counselor rephrases (slight rewording) what the client says.
>
> Level 3: Counselor paraphrases (inferring meaning, reflecting feelings, using analogies and metaphors, offering empathy) what the client says.

4. **Affirmations:** Affirmations are statements of appreciation and acknowledgment of the client's strengths, talents, and skills. Affirmations can encourage the development of self-efficacy. Using affirmations is a way to let clients know you hear and appreciate their efforts toward change.

5. **Summaries:** Summaries are forms of reflection that highlight the main points of the counselor-client interaction. Using summaries allows the clinician to direct clients to move toward change and provides information for clients as they go through this process. A counselor can conduct mini-summaries, session summaries, and transitional summaries.

6. **Change talk:** Change talk refers to statements clients make that express their reasons for making a change and that reinforce their thoughts about, the benefits of, and their commitments to change. Change talk statements include those related to clients' desires, ability, reasons, and needs to change as well as their commitments to change.[2] The counselor elicits change talk using the desires, abilities, reasons, and needs of the clients as well as capitalizing on clients' important values and strengths. From there, the counselor attends to clients' readiness for moving toward change. As clients talk more and more about change, what they might change, how they might change, and when change will happen for them, the more likely it becomes that the clients will actually change. There are additional strategies that work with the concept of change talk, such as exploring goals and values and identifying pros and cons for change, and so on, which are explored more thoroughly in chapter 6 of the second edition of Miller and Rollnick's *Motivational Interviewing*.

The diagram below reflects the process for eliciting and reinforcing a client's change talk. Many counselors keep a copy of this diagram in their office to remind them of how to use the change talk strategy when they are working with clients.

MI Change Talk Strategy Process

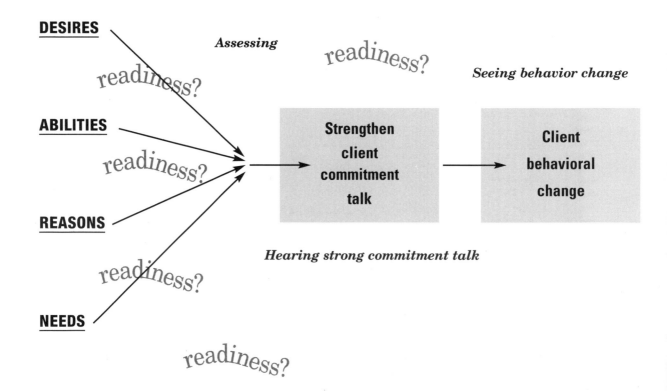

Asking for clients'

DESIRES

Assessing readiness?

readiness?

Seeing behavior change

ABILITIES

readiness?

Strengthen client commitment talk

Client behavioral change

REASONS

readiness?

Hearing strong commitment talk

NEEDS

readiness?

CLIENT VALUES   CLIENT STRENGTHS

Traps and Hazards

Miller and Rollnick have identified particular pitfalls, called "traps," in Phase 1 of Motivational Interviewing[3] and "hazards" in Phase 2.[4] They are listed below under the phase in which they most often occur. We've added tips or suggestions for counselors to help avoid these traps and hazards.

Phase 1 Traps

1. **Question/answer trap.**[5] In this common trap, counselors ask questions to get information, to fill silences, or to relieve their own anxiety. This approach is not useful in engaging clients, doesn't encourage communication or exploration, and can leave clients feeling not heard or cared for.

   T I P :
   Ask two to three open-ended questions for every closed-ended question.

2. **Taking a side trap.**[6] Most clients are ambivalent about change. Many professionals mistakenly support the most positive side of a client's ambivalence in hopes of convincing the client to choose it. However, taking a side will only reinforce the other or opposite side, usually a client's opposition to change. Counselors often assume they are responsible for convincing clients that change is better for them, and so they argue for it. This then absolves clients of their responsibility for exploring the positives of change and may unwittingly result in clients insisting on "no change" in reaction to the counselor's urgings.

   T I P :
   Remember to remain neutral. Use OARS to stay client-centered.

3. **Expert trap.**[7] The client, not the counselor, is the expert in MI counseling style. Counselors can easily get caught up in solving someone else's dilemma in the effort to be helpful. This leaves clients free of the responsibility of solving their own problems and in a position of finding the unsolicited advice never quite adequate. Hence, they don't have to change.

   T I P :
   Avoid a one-up, one-down relationship with clients. You have knowledge, but your knowledge is best used when clients ask for it as opposed to having it imposed on them.

4. **Labeling trap.**[8] Labeling a client's behavior can be judgmental or can reinforce a client's shame. Labeling is often not necessary and impedes exploration of the client's perspectives.

TIP:

Minimize the use of labels, including diagnostic labels,
by asking clients' perceptions about themselves.

5. **Premature focus trap.**[9] Counselors and clients may not have the same agendas for meetings. Forcing the counselor's agenda at the expense of being client-centered will result in the client's compliance, resistance, or lack of involvement. Eliciting change talk from and staying with clients—focusing on their needs, wants, wishes, and hopes—will often lead them to the agenda you may want to discuss with them. Timing and pacing are important. Your opinion of where clients are at and what they are ready for is secondary to theirs.

TIP:

Remember to ask clients what they think they want to do first
and remember to ask for permission before giving advice.

6. **Blaming trap.**[10] When clients come into contact with helpers, they often are worried about whether they will be blamed for all their families' problems. Clients may be concerned that they are not in control or capable. Defining the role of the helper relationship, clarifying what is going to happen in the process and what, if any, interpretations will be made will help avoid unnecessary defensiveness around feeling blamed. It is important to attend to this issue within the first couple of meetings.

TIP:

Emphasize to clients that counseling will be based on a collaboration between you
and them. What happens in counseling validates their strengths and abilities.

Guide to Phase 2 Motivational Interviewing Concepts

1. **Assess readiness:** Accurately assessing readiness for change helps direct the counselor's interventions appropriately. It reduces resistance and increases confidence and motivation for change.

2. **Transitional summary and key questions:** Summarizing the client's progress, decisions made, and skills attained, followed by a key open-ended question, continues to reinforce movement toward change.

3. **Information and advice:** Strategically used, offering information and advice can be helpful when clients request help or are ready to receive suggestions from the counselor.

4. **Negotiation of change planning:** Creating successful change plans involves assisting clients to consider what they think will work for them while pointing out potential challenges. It includes helping them problem solve and adjust their plans accordingly.

Phase 2 Hazards

1. **Overprescription.**[11] Once clients verbalize readiness to change, counselors may be tempted to make ambitious and non-client-centered change plans for them. Clients will erect verbal or behavioral barriers when the change plan reflects the counselor's agenda rather than their own. Clients may say, "I am ready to change. I am tired of this problem and want to do something new." We may counter with what we think is best for them, without considering their own solutions to their dilemmas.

TIP:
Start the process of planning for change by using OARS.
Reflections can be extremely helpful in staying on track with clients.
Monitor yourself to maintain the focus on the client's goals for treatment.

2. **Underestimating ambivalence.**[12] When a client starts showing signs of wanting to change, the counselor may assume that the client no longer has ambivalent feelings and *will* begin to change. This assumption may be inaccurate. The client may still have some ambivalence, although his confusion may not be as intense as it was in the earlier stages of change. Ignoring the client's real but less apparent ambivalence will inhibit movement toward change.

TIP:

Continue to assess client readiness for change.

3. **Insufficient Direction.**[13] People engaging in change may need guidance and assistance to make the desired change. Not providing this assistance because you are being "nondirective" and "client-centered" is not helpful when clients may be ready to move but are unsure of what to do next and want advice and information.

TIP:

If clients ask for advice, give it to them.

Stages of Change Guide to Practice

Precontemplation: Not Motivated, Confident, or Ready to Change

During this stage of change, people do not see that they have a substance use or abuse problem. Often, others are more concerned about them than they are about themselves. The clinician's job is to validate the client's view and see if the client is interested in looking further into why others may be concerned. It is important to attend to clients, building rapport to enable discussions of discrepancies between their values and beliefs. It is important to ask permission to discuss these issues. This should be done more than once, depending on the degree of client resistance the counselor experiences during counseling sessions.

Goals: Raise awareness, educate, create doubt, collaborate, and build trust.

Contemplation: Ambivalent, Low Confidence, Unsure about Change

As clients warm up to the idea of change as a positive, they often experience a period of ambivalence in which they have mixed feelings about change. Part of them sees the need for change, and another part of them does not. The clinician's job at this point in the process of change is to validate both sides of clients' ambivalence and assist them to make changes consistent with who they are and what is important to them, being sure to assess the role of substances in their life based on those important values and goals.

Goals: Build motivation and confidence to decide to change, strengthen commitment toward change.

Preparation: Motivated, Confident, Ready to Change

As clients resolve their ambivalence, the preparation stage of change becomes a time for them to plan for the change(s) they intend to make. This includes identifying in behavioral terms what they are going to change, what support they need to change, how to resolve barriers that come up, and how to implement their plans. It is important for the clinician to provide feedback and advice on creating realistic plans for change that will lead to success rather than frustration and failure. Building self-efficacy for change and reinforcing motivation to continue to engage in plans to change is essential during the counseling process.

Goal: Help client develop plans for change.

Action: Changing, Building Confidence

During the action phase of change, clients are carrying out their change plans. If the preparation stage of change has been done well, clients should be experiencing success and a measure of fulfillment as they make their desired changes. The clinician's role is to support their successes while acting as a resource for ongoing problem solving and barrier reduction. Clinicians may have to remind clients that they are making progress and affirm their motivation and successes, especially if clients experience unresolved ambivalence during this stage.

Goals: Affirm changes, monitor ambivalence,
problem solve barriers, and provide support.

Maintenance: Maintaining Changes, Affirming

This stage involves maintaining change and working through relapses, if they occur. As clients experience success and establish changes for themselves, the next decision point becomes monitoring how to maintain change and avoid triggers to return to old behaviors. Some may begin to think they can control their use or stay sober around using friends, or they may feel stress and then think drinking is going to soothe their stress without causing consequences. The clinician's job is to focus clients on their ongoing progress and remind them of the triggers that may get in the way of lasting success. Affirming their successes while reminding them of the reasons they decided to change are counselor goals for this stage of change.

Goals: Monitor progress, plan for relapse
prevention, reinforce commitment to action.

Processes of Change

The Processes of Change distinguish what happens to people as they change their behavior. The letters *E* and *B* following the name of each process indicate whether the process is mostly related to *experience* (experiencing an event in a way that creates a new way of thinking and feeling that leads to change) or *behavior* (engaging in activities that reinforce the changes people are making) or both.

1. **Consciousness raising** *(E)*

   A person becomes aware, which requires him to learn something new about behaviors that need to be changed.

2. **Social liberation** *(E, B)*

   A person recognizes changes in society that make it easier to follow through with the changes she is personally making or wants to make.

3. **Emotional arousal** *(E)*

   A person experiences an intensely charged event that results in movement toward change.

4. **Self-reevaluation** (E)

   A person experiences something that causes him to reflect on personal goals and values related to his use of substances.

5. **Stimulus control** *(B)*

   A person learns to manage barriers to change, such as triggers, and develops new coping skills to maintain change.

6. **Helping relationships** *(E, B)*

   A person identifies a variety of supportive people to help reinforce the desired changes.

7. **Reinforcement management** *(B)*

   A person regularly celebrates progress toward change.

8. **Counterconditioning** *(B)*

   A person chooses new ways to behave and interact to support the desired change.

9. **Self-liberation** *(B)*

   A person creates a plan that moves her to permanent change.

10. **Environmental reevaluation** *(E)*

    A person evaluates how his use affects home, friends, work, and other lifestyle areas.

Stages of Change At-a-Glance Sheets

The At-a-Glance sheets that follow were developed for counselors to use in family, individual, or group settings. They are particularly helpful for counselors who are in the process of integrating MI/SOC concepts to use during counseling sessions. Since there is a lot to remember when actually conducting a session, the information on the sheets reminds counselors of what to look for when working with clients. Often, counselors return to old patterns or habits. The sheets help them to keep on track with this new approach.

There is a separate At-a-Glance sheet for each stage of change. Each sheet contains the definition of and therapeutic goals for the stage, possible strategies to use, and examples of questions that can help elicit change talk. At-a-Glance sheets can be effective tools to take into sessions with clients by helping counselors understand their client's stage of change, determine the goal for the stage they assess their client to be in, and pick strategies that are best suited to the client they are seeing, being sure to assess the client's readiness to change. For example, a counselor may assess a client as being in the precontemplation stage of change. The counselor sees that one of the goals for precontemplation is to raise the client's awareness of the impact of his substance use on himself and others. The counselor looks at the various strategies on the precontemplation worksheet and decides to focus on establishing rapport and trust before attempting to offer factual information. At this point, the counselor has to rely on her knowledge about how to establish rapport and trust, and may recall the effectiveness of using OARS or other approaches.

Stimulating clients to verbalize their own thoughts and feelings about making changes is an important element of the change process. Therefore, at the bottom of the At-a-Glance sheets are lists of sample questions counselors can use during sessions to elicit change talk from clients.

It is important to evaluate what stage of change a client is in and to have a sense of how ready a client is to change before determining which At-a-Glance sheet would be most useful during a session. If the client appears to be in the preparation stage of change, but during the session turns out to be in contemplation, it is easy to switch focus by referring to both sheets. This allows counselors who are learning how SOC and MI work together to be flexible in meeting the counseling goals while attending to the needs of the client.

While the goal, strategies, and readiness assessment are determined, the counselor is also determining the best MI skills to apply, whether in Phase 1 or Phase 2, and matching them to the appropriate SOC. This is happening at the same time the counselor is maintaining the therapeutic relationship necessary to the ongoing engagement and retention of clients in the treatment process.

AT A GLANCE

Precontemplation Stage of Change

Stage Description

The client does not think there is a problem and is unlikely to engage in a change process.

Goals

Raise awareness of risks and problems. Respect and empathize with client's choices. Help the client engage in the counseling process and begin considering patterns and potential effects of his substance use.

Strategies

- Establish rapport and build trust.

- Explore and "decontaminate" the referral process.

- Affirm client for willingness to attend and talk.

- Explore the meaning of the events that brought the client to treatment.

- Elicit the client's perceptions of his behaviors and the larger situation.

- Offer factual information about the risks of substance use.

- Provide personalized feedback about assessment findings.

- Explore the good things and less good things about use.

- Express concern and "keep the door open."

- Raise doubts or concerns in the client about substance use by helping a significant other intervene.

- Raise doubts or concerns in the client about substance use by examining discrepancies between the client's and others' perceptions of the problem behavior.

Questions Helpful in Eliciting Change Talk

- What would need to be different in your life for you to consider making a change?

- Let's suppose you're considering making a change. Why would you want to do it?

- What do you like about your current behavior? What do you dislike?
- What would have to happen to you for you to consider making a change? How could I help you get there?
- What things make you think that this is a problem?
- What difficulties have you had in relation to your drug use?
- In what ways do you think your using or drinking has harmed you or others?
- In what ways has this been a problem for you?
- What is there about your drinking or using that you or others might see as reasons for concern?
- What worries do you have about your use?
- What do you think will happen if you stay the same?
- Would you be interested in knowing more about _____?
- Have you ever thought about changing?
- Would you like some information to read at home?

AT A GLANCE

Contemplation Stage of Change

Stage Description

The client acknowledges concerns and is considering the possibility of change but is ambivalent and uncertain.

Goals

Help the client see the "big picture" and discover discrepancies between her current behavior and her goals for the future. Assist the client to consider making some lifestyle change and build motivation and confidence to change.

Strategies

- Normalize ambivalence.
- Help the client tip the decisional balance scales toward change by
  - eliciting and weighing the pros and cons of continuing substance use versus discontinuing or changing use patterns
  - examining the client's personal values in relation to change
  - imagining the future looking forward and looking back
  - emphasizing the client's free choice, responsibility, and self-efficacy for change.
- Elicit self-motivational statements of intent and commitment from the client.
- Elicit ideas regarding the client's expectations of treatment.
- Summarize self-motivational statements.
- Assess client's sense of importance and confidence in changing.

Questions Helpful in Eliciting Change Talk

- What are some things you like about your current behavior? Is there anything you dislike?
- What are some reasons you would want things to stay just the way they are?
- What are some reasons for making a change?
- Imagine you decided to change. What would it be like? Why might you want to do it?

- Suppose some miracle happened, and you suddenly stopped your current behavior. How would you feel? How would your life be different? How would you handle difficult situations?

- When were you most successful in making a change? How did you do it?

- Where do we go from here? (Ask after spending sufficient time exploring ambivalence.)

AT A GLANCE

Preparation Stage of Change

Stage Description

The client is committed to change and is planning to make a change in the near future but is still considering what to do.

Goal

Help the client get ready to make a change by facilitating the development of a plan for change. Assist and guide the process by offering information and advice when requested by the client or when it best serves the client and his planning process.

Strategies

- Clarify the client's own goals and strategies for change.
- Offer a menu of options for change or treatment.
- With permission, offer expertise and advice.
- Negotiate a change—or treatment—plan and behavior contract.
- Consider and reduce barriers to change.
- Help the client enlist social support.
- Explore treatment expectancies and the client's role.
- Elicit from the client what has worked in the past either for him or for others he knows.
- Assist the client to negotiate finances, child care, work, transportation, or other potential barriers.
- Have the client publicly announce plans to change.

Questions Helpful in Eliciting Change Talk

- What are your main reasons for making this change?
- What do you think needs to change? What do you think would work?
- What are your ideas for making a change?
- If you gaze into the future after you have made the change, what kinds of things will you see yourself doing?

- There are probably a lot of things you could do. What do you think would really work for you?

- I can tell you what has worked for others in your situation, but what do you think would work best for you?

- What roadblocks might you encounter in making this change? How would you handle them?

- What kind of support do you have (family, friends, others) that can help you with your plan?

AT A GLANCE

Action Stage of Change

Stage Description

The client is actively taking steps to change but has not yet reached a stable state.

Goals

Assist the client in implementing her plan for change. Assist in resolving any barriers toward change, problem solve, and revise change plans as needed.

Strategies

- Engage the client in treatment and reinforce the importance of remaining in the change process.
- Support a realistic view of change through small steps.
- Acknowledge difficulties for the client in early stages of change.
- Help the client identify high-risk situations through a functional analysis and develop appropriate coping strategies to overcome these.
- Assist the client in finding new reinforcers of positive change.
- Help the client assess whether she has strong family and social support for change.

Questions Helpful in Reinforcing Change Talk

- What barriers have you encountered as you have taken steps toward change?
- How have you managed those barriers? What solutions have worked?
- Have you experienced a resurgence of ambivalence since you started working on your plan?
- What successes do you feel especially pleased about or proud of?
- What parts of your plan do you think need to be adjusted or eliminated for you to be successful at reaching your change goals?
- Is there anything you encountered while completing your process of change that you would like more information about?
- Is there an area in which you would like more support from others?

AT A GLANCE

Maintenance Stage of Change

Stage Description

The client has achieved initial goals and is now working to maintain gains.

Goals

Reinforce the client's successes. Establish and reinforce coping plans to handle triggers and the client's new lifestyle changes.

Strategies

- Help the client identify new reinforcers for behavior change.

- Support lifestyle changes.

- Affirm the client's resolve and self-efficacy.

- Help the client practice and use new coping strategies to avoid a return to old behaviors.

- Maintain supportive contact (e.g., explain to the client that you are available to talk between sessions).

- Develop a "fire escape" plan if the client returns to old behavior.

- Review long-term goals with the client.

Questions Helpful in Maintaining Change Talk

- When you look back on your recent success in accomplishing your plan, how would you describe your success to yourself or others?

- If you have experienced urges to resume your old behaviors, what coping strategies have proven to be useful?

- If you have experienced a recurrence of your old behaviors, how have you worked with it so that you do not lose the gains you already made?

- What do you consider the most valuable skills you have learned from this experience?

- Are there other changes you would like to pursue as a result of experiencing this current change? If so, what are they?

- How would you describe your present sense of confidence in your ability to make further changes now that you have succeeded in this experience?

AT A GLANCE

Maintenance—Relapse and Recycling

Stage Description

The client has experienced a recurrence of symptoms and must now cope with consequences and decide what to do next.

Goals

Assist client in relapse prevention or processing a relapse.

Strategies

- Help the client reenter the change cycle and commend any willingness to reconsider positive change.

- Explore the meaning and reality of the recurrence as a learning opportunity.

- Assist the client in finding alternative coping strategies.

- Maintain supportive contact.

Questions Helpful in Reestablishing Change Talk

- What led you to experience a return to the old behavior patterns?

- How did you manage to get back to where you want to be?

- How would you describe what you have learned from this experience?

- How would you describe your desire to continue to address the changes you identified?

- How would you describe your need to continue to address the changes you identified?

- What would you say are your reasons for continuing to address the changes you identified?

- How would you describe your confidence in your ability to continue to address the changes you identified?

- As you think about where you initially started and what you have learned through your process of making changes, what would you like to tell others in similar positions?

- How did you recapture your hope for change?

AGENCY IMPLEMENTATION PLANNING

In the next several pages, the reader will see two documents. The first is an Implementation Plan Development Checklist that details the key components of planning for and implementing best practice technology in existing organizations. The second document consists of two parts; the first part is a discussion of the sample plan, and the second part is the actual plan. The agency that developed the sample plan is called the Mid-Columbia Center for Living. The plan contains steps to incorporate best practices into their existing treatment program.

Creating a plan for a treatment focus change requires some forethought. Addressing issues such as why the change is needed, what the objectives for the change are, and how the agency will move toward the desired change increases the likelihood that the change will occur and be sustaining and effective. Adequate planning for change includes evaluating outcomes that demonstrate the change is working, is successful, and can be built on for future goals.

Our implementation plan is meant to be agency, administrator, and counselor friendly. Many times counselors create the impetus for change in social services agencies. Support for change is enhanced when the agency adopts a team approach. The implementation plan checklist should be straight forward for counselor use, yet comprehensive enough to meet the needs of the administrators and others whose jobs include implementation efforts.

Once the plan is conceived and begun, it is important to highlight successful steps along the way. Acknowledging positive progress reinforces the desired changes that have been made and motivates staff to work toward completing other changes specified in the plan. Staff involvement in planning is critical.

Duplicating this page is illegal. Do not copy this material without written permission from the publisher.

211

Activities such as in-service training, realistic client-focused case staffing, and recognition of the effects of change on counselors and their work are important. The reader can see that the Implementation Plan Development Checklist addresses many of the components that make a plan effective.

In the Mid-Columbia Center for Living MI Implementation Plan included in the Sample Implementation Plan document, some of the goals imply certain expectations for the agency. For example, goal number 4, "To support Best Practices and Outcomes through the support for staff certification and training, and improved data collection in the next two to four years," indicates that staff will need to be trained and increase their certification to accomplish the goals of the agency. For the counselors, this means that they will be expected to accept training and, when indicated, work toward certification in order to be congruent with the planned changes in the direction of best practices. Some counselors may need to decide for themselves if they wish to move in that direction professionally. Either way, change is inevitable, either within or outside the organization.

Implementation Plan Development Checklist[1]

Following is a five-point checklist to help you develop an implementation plan for program changes. As you complete each step, check it off and move on to the next. Once you complete the checklist, you will have an implementation plan for program changes. Before you get started, take some time to obtain program information that will help you develop an implementation plan that meets your program needs.

_____ 1. **Provide reasons for making program changes.**

Clearly state the reasons for program changes so staff will understand why the changes are being made. In addition, program changes should be based on meeting client needs better and should be supported by data.

Reason 1:

_____

_____

Reason 2:

_____

_____

Reason 3:

_____

_____

Client Population	Client Needs Being Met	Client Needs Not Being Met	Data to Support Need for Program Changes

continued on other side

_____ 2. **Develop program goals.**

Develop program goals that are concrete, specific, observable, and measurable. Clearly stated program goals are key to (a) helping staff understand what will be accomplished with the changes and (b) monitoring the implementation of the program changes. *Note:* You may have fewer or additional program goals.

Goal 1:

_____

_____

Goal 2:

_____

_____

Goal 3:

_____

_____

Goal 4:

_____

_____

_____ 3. **Plan for change.**

Explain how the planned program changes may impact your staff and organization. To facilitate the successful implementation of program changes, respond to the following sample questions and address any potential issues that may impact your staff and organization. You may identify additional questions that are important to consider for your program.

continued on next page

SAMPLE QUESTIONS TO CONSIDER	RESPONSES
1. How will this change impact your overall program?	
2. How will this change impact the clients in your program?	
3. How will this change impact the staff in your program?	
4. What does staff need to implement the program changes (e.g., training, materials, and free time to implement the changes)?	
5. How will staff needs be met (e.g., in-house trainings, free materials)?	
6. Will staff be offered incentives to make the changes (e.g., CEUs, reduced workloads)?	
7. What policies and procedures will need to be followed or implemented for this program to occur?	
8. How will this change impact the clients and others who use your program?	

continued on other side

_____ **4. Develop an implementation plan.**

Your implementation plan should include two elements: (a) the steps needed to implement the program changes and (b) a timeline for implementing the program changes. First, considering the information you provided on the previous page, identify three to five steps you will have to take to implement the program changes. Then create a timeline for implementation.

STEPS	TIME FRAME (e.g., weeks, months)
Step 1:	
Step 2:	
Step 3:	
Step 4:	
Step 5:	

_____ **5. Review final considerations.**

Successful implementation of program changes involves (a) clear communication with staff regarding the reasons for change, the planned changes, and how the changes will be implemented; (b) clear presentation of program goals; and (c) follow-through with commitment to provide the needed supportive services to staff in order to implement the changes. Take a moment to review the previous points. Make sure you have thoroughly thought through what it takes to implement the desired program changes. Last, consider how you can evaluate the implementation of the program changes.

Sample Implementation Plan

Following is an actual plan that was written by the director of substance abuse and mental health services of Hood River County, Oregon, for Mid-Columbia Center for Living (MCCFL), an agency that serves the mental health and substance abuse needs of the rural community of Hood River County. It was developed in order to implement Motivational Interviewing and Stages of Change into the organization's clinical practice. The agency director has permitted us to use this plan as an example of the type of planning and detail needed when contemplating change in organizational life. It reflects concepts identified previously in the Implementation Plan Development Checklist.

As you read the plan that follows, you may want to reflect on your own agency. Here are some questions to consider:

1. How would you write a plan that addresses the integration of MI/SOC into your agency's clinical practice?

2. What are the issues confronting your community, and thus your agency, that impact changes in your agency?

3. If you are a counselor, what are the issues you see that would support you in implementing MI/SOC? Is there a way for you to communicate those needs to your agency management? If so, how?

4. How do you see improving your skills in your practice as new technologies are identified and the standard of practice for your clients changes over time?

Answering these and other questions will aid you in your practice and provide the important clinical structures for you and the people you serve.

Mid-Columbia Center for Living MI Implementation Plan[2]

The goals set forth in the Mid-Columbia Center for Living (MCCFL) MI Implementation Plan for 1999–2001 and recently updated are as follows:

1. To support the Institute of Medicine Model in all facets of service delivery and to promote adequate funding for all services, including Level III care. This is a long-term goal of two to six years.

2. To continue to participate with other community partners to provide a

Duplicating this page is illegal. Do not copy this material without written permission from the publisher.

217

local and regional response to the challenges set forth in the SAFE Families Act and Welfare-to-Work.

3. To expand on the foundation recently established for the provision of transitional housing in the Mid-Columbia and across the region. Within the next two years, acquire property to complete construction for single-family units in the Mid-Columbia.

4. To support Best Practices and Outcomes through the support for staff certification and training, and improved data collection in the next two to four years.

A related goal, identified in the past year, is to implement an electronic clinical record-keeping system, Anasazi, which will incorporate Best Practices in the assessment and treatment-planning components.

The specific strategies identified to meet the Best Practices goal include

A. *ASAM PPC-II-R:* MCCFL uses the current Oregon version of ASAM placement criteria and *DSM-IV* to determine need for treatment as well as intensity of services. All staff will be trained in application of PPC-II-R in the next year (2002). We will also be advocating for regional trainings, with at least one of these to be in the eastern Oregon region and provided by Dr. Mee-Lee.

B. *Staff training:* MCCFL has made, and will continue to make, a strong commitment to staff training and skill enhancement with specific focus on

   1. ASAM/PPC-II-R

   2. Co-occurring disorders

   3. Motivational Interviewing/Stages of Change

   4. Anasazi record keeping

C. *Certification:* MCCFL treatment staff are certified through ACCBO or NAADAC. We are also planning to implement new contract language for the subcontracted prevention services that includes requirements for staff/coordinator certification and Letter of Approval for service providers. We believe that certification is an important component of Best Practices and Outcomes.

D. *IOM:* By subscribing to the Institute of Medicine Model, we are in support of the continuum spanning universal prevention, case identification, targeted prevention, treatment, and aftercare.

E. *Outcomes:* Treatment outcomes are a vital component of Best Practices. Therefore, we are planning the allocation of resources (through clinical supervision and Quality Assurance/Quality Improvement) to measure the effectiveness of these planned strategies.

The schedule of activities and timelines for addressing A and B is

JANUARY–FEBRUARY

1. Review staff training experiences in MI; identify those who have not had MI training in the past one to two years.

2. Identify a "common language" and model for communicating about MI. Begin prompting use of language in monthly case presentation/peer review. (This is a new QA/QI exercise, suggested by staff, hence it will lend itself to formatting in the MI/SOC language).

3. Identify spring training(s).

4. Work with Anasazi work group to advocate inclusion of SOC in Dimension 4 component of the assessment protocol.

MARCH

1. Provide an in-house training, cosponsored with Morrow-Wheeler-Grant Behavioral Health, Inc.

2. Include a comparison of current practices regarding assessment of SOC and treatment plan interventions with the future model, which demonstrates the MI Best Practices applications in assessment, treatment plans, and individual and group treatment strategies.

MAY

1. Staff will attend Dr. Mee-Lee's ASAM/PPC-II-R training in Boardman, which will include a hands-on practical application component of the theory presented.

2. Begin utilizing the MI skill set in clinical assessment and treatment planning.

JUNE

1. Case presentations at staffings will include demonstration and support for application of the MI Best Practices.

    Staff would be apprised of this 2002 Implementation Plan Update in early January. The plan will be reviewed in monthly team meetings to provide opportunity for feedback, evaluation, and revisions.

■ ■ ■

RESOURCES

Internet Web Sites

Following is a list of substance abuse-related prevention and treatment Web sites containing research results, materials that can be ordered at no cost, and links to other useful sites.

Addiction Technology Transfer Center
 www.nattc.org

Cancer Prevention Research Center at the University of Rhode Island
 www.uri.edu/research/cprc/transtheoretical.htm

Center for Mental Health Services (CMHS) Knowledge Exchange Network (KEN)
 www.mentalhealth.org/

Center for Substance Abuse Prevention
 www.samhsa.gov/centers/csap/csap.html

Center for Substance Abuse Treatment
 www.samhsa.gov/csat/csat.htm

Motivational Interviewing
 www.motivationalinterview.org

National Clearinghouse for Alcohol and Drug Information (NCADI) Catalog of Publications of the Substance Abuse and Mental Health Services Administration, U.S. Department of Health and Human Services
 http://store.health.org/

National Institute on Alcohol Abuse and Alcoholism (NIAAA)
 www.niaaa.nih.gov

National Institute on Drug Abuse
 www.nida.nih.gov

National Institutes of Health

www.nih.gov/

National Substance Abuse Web Index

http://nsawi.health.org

Substance Abuse and Mental Health Services Administration (SAMHSA)

www.samhsa.gov

Motivational Interviewing Videotapes

Miller, W. R., S. Rollnick, and T. B. Moyers. *Motivational Interviewing.* Albuquerque, N.Mex.: Center on Alcoholism, Substance Abuse, and Addictions (CASAA), University of New Mexico, 1998. A six-part series of training videos available in VHS cassette format.

Articles and Publications

For articles and other publications, please see the bibliography on pages 227–29.

■ ■ ■

NOTES

Chapter 1: Fundamentals

1. M. J. Lambert, D. A. Shapiro, and A. E. Bergin. 1986. The effectiveness of psychotherapy. In *Handbook of psychotherapy and behavior change,* 3d ed., ed. S. L. Garfield and A. E. Bergin, 157–212. New York: Wiley.

2. S. M. Varney, D. J. Rohsenow, A. N. Dey, M. G. Myers, W. R. Zwick, and P. M. Monti. 1995. Factors associated with help seeking and perceived dependence among cocaine users. *American Journal of Drug and Alcohol Abuse* 21 (1): 81–91; D. G. Kilpatrick, J. C. Roitzsch, C. L. Best, D. A. McAlhany, E. T. Sturgis, and W. C. Miller. 1978. Treatment goal preference and problem perception of chronic alcoholics: Behavioral and personality correlates. *Addictive Behaviors* 3:107–16; K. D. Charalamous, B. K. Ford, and T. J. Skinner. 1976. Self-esteem in alcoholics and nonalcoholics. *Journal of Studies on Alcohol* 37:990–94.

3. W. R. Miller and N. Heather, eds. 1998. *Treating addictive behaviors: Processes of change,* 2d ed., 325. New York: Plenum Press; A. A. Adinolfi, B. DiDario, and F. W. Kelso. 1981. The relationship between drinking patterns at therapy termination and intake and termination status on social variables: A replication study. *International Journal of the Addictions* 16:555–65; D. L. Strug and M. M. Hyman. 1981. Social networks of alcoholics. *Journal of Studies on Alcohol* 42:855–84.

4. L. C. Sobell, M. B. Sobell, T. Toneatto, and G. I. Leo. 1993. What triggers the resolution of alcohol problems without treatment? *Alcoholism: Clinical and Experimental Research* 17:217–24.

5. J. O. Prochaska. 1999. How do people change, and how can we change to help many more people? In *The heart and soul of change: What works in therapy,* ed. M. A. Hubble, S. D. Miller, and B. L. Duncan, 227–55. Washington, D.C.: American Psychological Association.

6. Project MATCH Research Group. 1998. Therapist effects in three treatments for alcohol problems. *Psychotherapy Research* 8:455–74.

7. L. M. Najavits and R. D. Weiss. 1994. Variations in therapist effectiveness in the treatment of patients with substance use disorders: An empirical review. *Addiction* 89 (6): 679–88; W. R. Miller, R. G. Benefield, and J. S. Tonigan. 1993. Enhancing motivation for change in problem drinking: A controlled comparison of two therapist styles. *Journal of Consulting and Clinical Psychology* 61:455–61; L. Luborsky, A. T. McLellan, G. E. Woody, C. P. O'Brien, and A. Auerback. 1985. Therapist success and its determinants. *Archives of General Psychiatry* 42:602–11.

8. H. A. Skinner and B. A. Allen. 1983. Differential assessment of alcoholism. *Journal of Studies on Alcohol* 44:852–62.

9. W. R. Miller and R. G. Sovereign. 1989. The check-up: A model for early intervention in addictive behaviors. In *Addictive behaviors: Prevention and early intervention,* ed. T. Loberg, W. R. Miller, P. E. Nathan, and G. A. Marlatt, 219–31. Amsterdam: Swets & Zeitlinger; G. R. Patterson and M. S. Forgatch. 1985. Therapist behavior as a determinant for client noncompliance: A paradox for the behavior modifier. *Journal of Consulting and Clinical Psychology* 53:846–51; W. R. Miller, R. G. Benefield, and J. S. Tonigan. 1993. Enhancing motivation for change in problem drinking: A controlled comparison of two therapist styles. *Journal of Consulting and Clinical Psychology* 61:455–61.

10. G. J. Leake and A. S. King. 1977. Effect of counselor expectations on alcoholic recovery. *Alcohol Health and Research World* 11 (3): 16–22.

11. Project MATCH Research Group. 1997. Matching alcoholism treatments to client heterogeneity: Project MATCH posttreatment drinking outcomes. *Journal of Studies on Alcohol* 58 (1): 7–29.

Chapter 2: Integrating Motivational Interviewing and Stages of Change

1. J. O. Prochaska, J. C. Norcross, and C. C. DiClemente. 1994. *Changing for good,* 36–50. New York: William Morrow and Co.

2. Center for Substance Abuse Treatment and Mental Health Services Administration. 1999. *Enhancing motivation for change in community substance abuse treatment programs.* Treatment Improvement Protocol (TIP) Series No. 35. W. R. Miller, Consensus Panel Chair.

3. W. F. Velicer, J. O. Prochaska, J. L. Fava, G. J. Norman, and C. A. Redding. 1998. Detailed overview of the Transtheoretical Model—smoking cessation and stress management: Applications of the Transtheoretical Model of behavior change. *Homeostasis* 38:216–33.

4. W. R. Miller and S. Rollnick. 1995. What is motivational interviewing? *Behavioural and Cognitive Psychotherapy: An International Multidisciplinary Journal for the Helping Professions* 23:325–34.

5. W. R. Miller and S. Rollnick. 2002. *Motivational interviewing: Preparing people for change,* 2d ed., 65. New York: Guilford Press.

6. Ibid., ch. 10.

7. Ibid., 37.

8. Ibid., 40.

9. Ibid., 76–79.

10. Ibid.

11. Ibid., 55–63.

12. Ibid., 128–32.

Chapter 3: Opening the Door to Change

1. Center for Substance Abuse Treatment and Mental Health Services Administration. 1999. *Enhancing motivation for change in community substance abuse treatment programs.* Treatment Improvement Protocol (TIP) Series No. 35, 31–32. W. R. Miller, Consensus Panel Chair.

2. W. R. Miller and S. Rollnick. 2002. *Motivational interviewing: Preparing people for change,* 2d ed., 16. New York: Guilford Press.

Chapter 4: Planning for and Implementing Change

1. Center for Substance Abuse Treatment and Mental Health Services Administration. 1999. *Enhancing motivation for change in community substance abuse treatment programs.* Treatment Improvement Protocol (TIP) Series No. 35, 31–32. W. R. Miller, Consensus Panel Chair.

Chapter 5: Maintaining Change

1. Center for Substance Abuse Treatment and Mental Health Services Administration. 1999. *Enhancing motivation for change in community substance abuse treatment programs.* Treatment Improvement Protocol (TIP) Series No. 35, 31–32. W. R. Miller, Consensus Panel Chair.

Chapter 6: Special Populations

1. R. Drake, K. Mercer-McFadden, C. T. Meuser, G. J. McHugo, and G. R. Bond. 1998. Review of integrated mental health and substance abuse treatment for patients with dual diagnosis. *Schizophrenia Bulletin* 24 (4): 589–608.

2. Substance Abuse and Mental Health Services Administration, U.S. Department of Health and Human Services. 2002. *Report to Congress on the prevention and treatment of co-occurring substance abuse disorders and mental disorders,* i, 108. 2 December; Centre for Addiction and Mental Health. 2002. *Best practices: Concurrent mental health and substance use disorders,* 15, 175. Ottawa, Ont.: Health Canada.

3. F. Osher and L. L. Kofoed. 1989. Treatment of patients with psychiatric and psychoactive substance abuse disorders. *Hospital and Community Psychiatry* 40:1025–30.

4. K. van Wormer and D. R. Davis. 2003. *Addictions treatment: A strengths perspective,* 258. Pacific Grove, Calif.: Wadsworth.

Chapter 7: Putting Motivational Interviewing and Stages of Change into Practice

1. D. Mee-Lee, L. Gartner, M. M. Miller, G. Shulman, and B. B. Wilford. 1998. *Patient placement criteria for the treatment of substance-related disorders* (PPC-2). 2d ed. Ed. B. B. Wilford. Chevy Chase, Md.: American Society of Addiction Medicine.

Appendix A: Guide to Practice and At-a-Glance Sheets

1. W. R. Miller and S. Rollnick. 2002. *Motivational interviewing: Preparing people for change,* 2d ed., 65. New York: Guilford Press.

2. P. C. Amrhein, W. R. Miller, C. E. Yahne, M. Palmer, and L. Fulcher. 2003. Client commitment language during motivational interviewing predicts drug use outcomes. *Journal of Consulting and Clinical Psychology* 71:862–78.

3. W. R. Miller and S. Rollnick. 2002. *Motivational interviewing: Preparing people for change,* 2d ed., 55–63. New York: Guilford Press.

4. Ibid., 128–29.

5. Ibid., 55.

6. Ibid., 56.

7. Ibid., 60.

8. Ibid.

9. Ibid., 62.

10. Ibid., 63.

11. Ibid., 129.

12. Ibid., 128.

13. Ibid., 129.

Appendix B: Agency Implementation Planning

1. S. W. Hayashi and J. Y. Huang. 2002. *Implementation plan checklist.* Silver Spring, Md.: Johnson, Bassin & Shaw, Inc. (301) 495-1080. The development of this checklist was supported by contract 270-97-7005 from the Center for Substance Abuse Treatment, Substance Abuse and Mental Health Services Administration, Department of Health and Human Services.

2. D. Mason. 1999. *Mid-Columbia Center for Living MI Implementation Plan.* The Dalles, Oreg.: Mid-Columbia Center for Living.

■ ■ ■

BIBLIOGRAPHY

Amrhein, P. C., W. R. Miller, C. E. Yahne, M. Palmer, and L. Fulcher. 2003. Client commitment language during motivational interviewing predicts drug use outcomes. *Journal of Consulting and Clinical Psychology* 71:862–78.

Bandura, A. 1994. Self-efficacy. In *Encyclopedia of human behavior,* vol. 4, ed. V. S. Ramachaudran, 71–81. New York: Academic Press. (Reprinted in *Encyclopedia of mental health,* ed. H. Friedman. San Diego: Academic Press, 1998.)

Brann, S. 2000. *Cultural considerations: Making motivational interviewing work for different ethnic groups.* Resource Section, Tip 35 Curriculum.

Center for Substance Abuse Treatment and Mental Health Services Administration. 1994. *Assessment and treatment of patients with coexisting mental health and alcohol and other drug abuse.* Treatment Improvement Protocol (TIP) Series No. 9. R. Ries, M.D., Consensus Panel Chair.

———. 1999. *Enhancing motivation for change in community substance abuse treatment programs.* Treatment Improvement Protocol (TIP) Series No. 35. W. R. Miller, Consensus Panel Chair.

———. 1999. *Treatment of adolescents with substance use disorders.* Treatment Improvement Protocol (TIP) Series. No. 32–33. K. Winters, Ph.D., Consensus Panel Chair.

———. 2000. *The change book: A blueprint for technology transfer.* Kansas City, Mo.: Addiction Technology Transfer Center (ATTC).

Centre for Addiction and Mental Health. 2002. *Best practices: concurrent mental health and substance use disorders.* Ottawa, Ont.: Health Canada.

DiClemente, C. C. 2003. *Addiction and change: How addictions develop and addicted people recover.* New York: Guilford Press.

Drake, R., C. Mercer-McFadden, K. T. Meuser, G. J. McHugo, and G. R. Bond. 1998. Review of integrated mental health and substance abuse treatment for patients with dual diagnosis. *Schizophrenia Bulletin* 24 (4): 589–608.

Evans, K., and J. M. Sullivan. 1990. *Dual diagnosis: Counseling the mentally ill substance abuser.* New York: Guilford Press.

Freeman, A., and M. Dolan. 2001. Revising Prochaska and DiClemente's Stages of Change theory: An expansion and specifications to aid in treatment planning and outcome evaluation. *Cognitive and Behavior Practice* 8:224–34.

Gordon, T. 1975. *Parent effectiveness training.* New York: Plume.

Ingersoll, K. S., C. C. Wagner, and S. Gharib. 2000. *Motivational groups for community substance abuse programs.* Richmond, Va.: Mid-Atlantic Addiction Technology Transfer Center. www.mid-attc.org

Longshore, D., C. Grills, K. Annon, and R. Grady. 1998. Promoting recovery from drug abuse: An Africentric intervention. *Journal of Black Psychology* 28 (3): 319–33.

Longshore, D., and C. Grills. 2000. Motivating illegal drug use recovery: Evidence for a culturally congruent intervention. *Journal of Black Psychology* 26 (3): 288–301.

Marlatt, G. A. 1998. *Harm reduction: Pragmatic strategies of managing high-risk behaviors.* New York: Guilford Press.

Mee-Lee, D., L. Gartner, M. M. Miller, G. Shulman, and B. B. Wilford. 1998. *Patient placement criteria for the treatment of substance-related disorders* (PPC-2). 2d ed. Ed. B. B. Wilford. Chevy Chase, Md.: American Society of Addiction Medicine.

Miller, W. R. 1985. Motivation for treatment: A review with special emphasis on alcoholism. *Psychological Bulletin* 98:84–107.

———. 1989. Matching individuals with interventions. In *Handbook of alcoholism treatment approaches: Effective alternatives,* ed. R. K. Hester and W. R. Miller, 261–71. Elmsford, N.Y.: Pergamon Press.

———. 1996. Motivational interviewing: Research, practice, and puzzles. *Addictive Behaviors* 21 (6): 835–42.

———. 2002. A streetcar named desire. *Motivational Interviewing Newsletter for Trainers* 9 (3). www.motivationalinterview.org

Miller, W. R., and T. F. Pechacek. 1987. New roads: Assessing and treating psychological dependence. *Journal of Substance Abuse Treatment* 4:73–77.

Miller, W. R., A. Zweben, C. DiClemente, and R. Rychtarik. 1995. *Motivational enhancement therapy manual: A clinical research guide for therapists treating individuals with alcohol abuse and dependence.* Project MATCH Monograph Series, vol. 2. NIH Publication No. 94. Rockville, Md.: National Institute on Alcohol Abuse and Alcoholism.

Miller, W. R., and S. Rollnick. 1991. *Motivational interviewing: Preparing people to change addictive behavior.* New York: Guilford Press.

———. 1995. What is motivational interviewing? *Behavioural and Cognitive Psychotherapy: An International Multidisciplinary Journal for the Helping Professions* 23:325–34.

———. 2002. *Motivational interviewing: Preparing people for change.* 2d ed. New York: Guilford Press.

Monti, P., S. Colby, and T. O'Leary, eds. 2001. *Adolescents, alcohol, and substance abuse: Reaching teens through brief interventions.* New York: Guilford Press.

Osher, F., and L. L. Kofoed. 1989. Treatment of patients with psychiatric and psychoactive substance abuse disorders. *Hospital and Community Psychiatry* 40:1025–30.

Prochaska, J. O., J. C. Norcross, and C. C. DiClemente. 1994. *Changing for good.* New York: William Morrow and Co.

Project MATCH Research Group. 1997. Matching alcoholism treatments to client heterogeneity: Project MATCH posttreatment drinking outcomes. *Journal of Studies on Alcohol* 58 (1): 23.

———. 1998. Therapist effects in three treatments for alcohol problems. *Psychotherapy Research* 8:455–74.

Rollnick, S., P. Mason, and C. Butler. 1999. *Health behavior change: A guide for practitioners.* Churchill Livingstone: Edinburgh.

Substance Abuse and Mental Health Services Administration, U.S. Department of Health and Human Services. 2002. *Report to Congress on the prevention and treatment of co-occurring substance abuse disorders and mental disorders.* 2 December.

Sue, D. 1990. *Counseling the culturally different: Theory and practice.* 2d ed. New York: John Wiley & Sons.

van Wormer, K., and D. R. Davis. 2003. *Addictions treatment: A strengths perspective.* Pacific Grove, Calif.: Wadsworth.

Velicer, W. F., J. O. Prochaska, J. L. Fava, G. J. Norman, and C. A. Redding. 1998. Detailed overview of the Transtheoretical Model—smoking cessation and stress management: Applications of the Transtheoretical Model of behavior change. *Homeostasis* 38:216–33.

White, W. L. 1998. *Slaying the dragon: The history of addiction treatment and recovery in America.* Bloomington, Ill.: Chestnut Health Systems.

■ ■ ■

Kathyleen M. Tomlin, M.S., L.P.C., C.A.D.C. III, is the clinical services manager at Kaiser Permanente Addiction Medicine: Adult, Adolescent and Family Chemical Dependency Services in Portland, Oregon. For nearly thirty years, she has worked in the addictions treatment and prevention field as a counselor, administrator, educator, and consultant. Since 1981, she has specialized in the treatment of adolescents who suffer from addiction and multiple DSM diagnoses, and their families. She has provided care in outpatient as well as residential settings. In addition to her work at Kaiser Permanente, Tomlin continues an active private practice in Portland as a writer, trainer, and consultant. Tomlin's most recent involvement is developing treatment programs geared toward those suffering from addiction with an emphasis on the use of Motivational Interviewing and Stages of Change theory.

Helen Richardson, B.S., has been active in the addictions field since 1970. She began her work as a volunteer at the Alcoholism Information Center in Saginaw, Michigan. As an employee, she worked with adults and adolescents as an educator, a counselor, and eventually the acting executive director until she moved to Portland, Oregon. There she became the executive director of Mainstream Youth Program, Inc., an outpatient adolescent treatment and prevention agency. During her thirteen-year tenure there, she conceptualized and implemented community-based service delivery at more than sixteen locations throughout the county and developed culturally appropriate treatment services for African American youth and their families. After a stint as director of Mulnomah County's Commission on Children and Families and another as a legislative assistant, she resumed her career in the chemical dependency field as a consultant, developing and delivering training and other services.

About the Publisher

Hazelden Publishing and Educational Services is a division of the Hazelden Foundation, a not-for-profit organization. Since 1949, Hazelden has been a leader in promoting the dignity and treatment of people afflicted with the disease of chemical dependency.

The mission of the foundation is to improve the quality of life for individuals, families, and communities by providing a national continuum of information, education, and recovery services that are widely accessible; to advance the field through research and training; and to improve our quality and effectiveness through continuous improvement and innovation.

Stemming from that, the mission of this division is to provide quality information and support to people wherever they may be in their personal journey—from education and early intervention, through treatment and recovery, to personal and spiritual growth.

Although our treatment programs do not necessarily use everything Hazelden publishes, our bibliotherapeutic materials support our mission and the Twelve Step philosophy upon which it is based. We encourage your comments and feedback.

The headquarters of the Hazelden Foundation are in Center City, Minnesota. Additional treatment facilities are located in Chicago, Illinois; Newberg, Oregon; New York, New York; Plymouth, Minnesota; St. Paul, Minnesota; and West Palm Beach, Florida. At these sites, we provide a continuum of care for men and women of all ages. Our Plymouth facility is designed specifically for youth and families.

For more information on Hazelden,
please call **1-800-257-7800.**

Or you may access our World Wide Web site
on the Internet at **www.hazelden.org.**